IMAGES OF WALES

MUMBLES AND GOWER PUBS

IMAGES OF WALES

MUMBLES AND GOWER PUBS

BRIAN E. DAVIES

To John & June,
with best wishes,
Brian Davies

TEMPUS

To Ted, my father, who would have approved

Frontispiece: The village of Oystermouth and Mumbles lighthouse photographed from Oystermouth Castle by Mary Dillwyn, *c.* 1850s. The White Rose Inn can be seen in the foreground.

First published 2006

Tempus Publishing Limited
The Mill, Brimscombe Port,
Stroud, Gloucestershire, GL5 2QG
www.tempus-publishing.com

British Library Cataloguing in Publication Data.
A catalogue record for this book is available from the British Library.

ISBN 0 7524 3779 8

Typesetting and origination by Tempus Publishing Limited.
Printed in Great Britain.

Contents

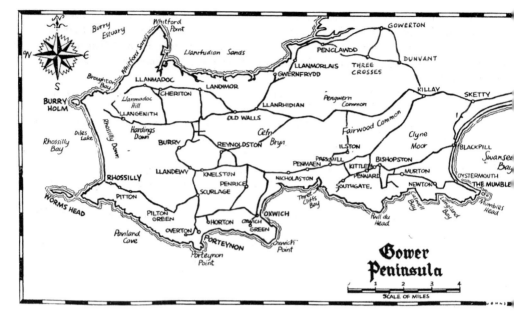

Map by Peter Johns, reproduced from *My Gower* by H.M. Tucker (published by Rowlands & Co., 1957).

Acknowledgements

Thanks to my wife Mari, for her help and patience, my daughter, Lucy, for her encouragement, and son, Phil, for his computer skills.

I am very grateful to the following for their invaluable assistance: Kim Collis and the staff of West Glamorgan Archive Service; Marilyn Jones and staff of Swansea Reference Library; Richard Brighton of the Cambrian Indexing Project;
Bernice Cardy and Michael Gibbs of Swansea Museum; Wendy Cope and members of Oystermouth Historical Association; The Bass Museum, Burton on Trent; the *Mumbles News* and Roger David Studios; Glamorgan Records Office; the Clare family; the Gower Society; Blackpill Local History Society; Gowerton Archive Group; Gowerton Community Council; John Howson of Veteran Records; Swansea and Neath CAMRA.

Also to: Dr Ronald L. Austin, Charlotte Bevan, Terry Bevan, Stan Bollom, Dr Angela M Brunt, Stuart Eley, Rory Gowland, Liz Grove, Alan Howells, S.C. Jeffery, Randolph Jenkins, Dr Wally Jenkins, Cyril John, Ann Jones and Roger Phillips Jones, Dr J.L. Jones, Grafton Maggs, Jan McKechnie, Bernard Morris, Peter Muxworthy, Derek Norton, Len O'Driscoll, Dr Geoffrey R. Orrin, Mervyn Owen, Jeremy Parkhouse, Timothy Perkins, Professor Paul Preece, Ken Reeves, Ann Roberts, Anna Stevens, Ted Summers, Hugh Thomas, 'Puss' Thomas and Jeff Towns.

Authors referred to include Rod Cooper, James A. Davies, Gareth Evans, Paul Ferris, Gerald Gabb, Gary Gregor, Heather Holt, Neville Jones, Robert Lucas, Carol Powell, David Rees, J. Hywel Rees, David Roberts, W.C. Rogers, Carl Smith, J. Mansel Thomas, Norman L. Thomas, Wynford Vaughan Thomas, Horatio M. Tucker and Pat Williams

Photographs have been kindly provided from many sources including: City & County of Swansea, Swansea Museum and Archive Service and by permission of Llyfrgell Genedlaethol Cymru/The National Library of Wales. Photograph of Daniel Jones by Bernard Mitchell and the South Pole photograph by Henry Bowers, from Canterbury Museum, New Zealand (ref 19XX.2.639)

I'd particularly like to thank the licensees, present and past, of Mumbles and Gower pubs, pub regulars and many, many others for their support and interest.

Information has been gathered from countless primary and secondary sources including licensing records, Ordnance Survey maps, the *Cambrian* and other old newspapers, the *Mumbles News*, census returns, tithe and estate records, parish records, guides, Gower Society Journals and many excellent books that have been written about this special corner of Wales. In addition, many recollections come from people I've met and talked to – there were some particularly good anecdotes. I've tried to acknowledge people who have helped, but it's not possible to include everybody or an exhaustive bibliography. Inevitably, inaccuracies may occur when thousands of bits of information are distilled into over 180 captions.

Introduction

On 4 December 1903, a speaker at the Oystermouth Temperance Federation in Mumbles stated that 'Drunkenness and its attendant sins are works of the Devil – the intemperance, insanity, suicide, debauches, crime and murder caused, result in poverty, shattered health, starvation, misery, early graves, a prison cell and often a scaffold – pray that the day will soon dawn when sin and Satan shall be cast into the bottomless pit for ever and ever'.

Whatever your view, the temperance campaigns of the Revivalist period certainly had an effect on the area's pubs. The Welsh Sunday Closing Act of 1881 had closed pubs in Wales on Sundays except for bona fide travellers, who were defined as people journeying more than three miles with a genuine need of refreshment. Every Sunday, people from Swansea flocked onto the Mumbles train and many descended on the pubs of Oystermouth, (which was conveniently over the three mile limit). The police in Mumbles had the impossible task of sorting out genuine travellers (few) from people who wanted to get drunk (many) and also Mumbles locals pretending to be travellers! The chapel-goers were up in arms. This became such an issue that the problem of the 'bona fide humbugs' was debated in the House of Commons, with Mumbles used as the prime example of abuse of the Act.

Drunkenness in Mumbles was nothing new. In 1866, during the height of the oyster boom, a visitor commented, 'drunkenness seems to be the bane of the village, vacancy of mind being the consequence'. The 'Mumbles Mile' was clearly in business a very long time ago!

Of course, thousands of people visited Mumbles because it was, and still is, a wonderful place to visit. From its distinctive lighthouse and famous Mumbles Pier, to the promenade and imposing

Oystermouth Castle – the place is simply irresistible. The Mumbles Railway opened in 1804 as first passenger railway in the world, and increasing numbers of people have been making the fiv mile journey from Swansea ever since.

But what of the pubs? Registers of alehouse recognizance were first required in 1753, when there were sixteen alehouses recorded in Oystermouth parish. Licensed *alehouses* were also able to sell wines and spirits, while *beerhouses* were limited to the sale of beer and cider. Many of the poorer Mumbles pubs were closed in the early 1900s due to the attention of the temperance movement and the desire of the police and licensing justices to reduce their number. The Compensation Act of 1904 softened the blow, with pub owners, breweries and licensees paid compensation for closure.

By contrast, pubs on the Gower Peninsula had a relatively peaceful time. There was plenty of barley for beer making and farmers often had their own brewhouses, some of which became established as cottage pubs. The 1750s saw no less than sixty-nine alehouses on the peninsula. Farmers, fishermen, mariners, weavers and quarrymen would all be found in the village taverns. Well-known fairs, such as Penrice, Reynoldston, Llanrhidian and Kittle, attracted large crowds to their sales with drovers, itinerant traders and wandering musicians adding to the colourful activi In addition, the Mapsant (Saint's Day) celebrations in the villages would often be rumbustious affairs with games, cock fights and prize-fighting tourneys going on (and much ale consumed ir the local inns). When you add the many and varied Gower customs to the mix (together with some smuggling and wrecking), you can imagine the scenes in many of the old pubs. Inevitably, there was a certain amount of pressure for pub closures from the non-conformists in rural Gow and the Penrice Estate obliged by allowing a number of inns to close in the nineteenth and earl twentieth centuries.

The history of the peninsula's pubs follows the course of the area's social history, with the arr of tourists in the late Victorian era interweaving with the traditions of the local communities. These were very different in rural 'English Gower' in the south and west from 'Welsh Gower' in north and east with its industrial activity, cockle-fishing and rugby playing. Many of Penclawdd' inns were closed in the early 1900s due to a combination of pressure from the police and justice together with the gradual decline of local industries, such as tinplate and coal mining.

Our journey takes us in a clockwise direction around Gower, starting at the Red Lion in Blackpill and ending at the Railway Inn, Upper Killay. Some eighty pubs are visited, around hal which are still in existence. We'll meet many characters, including Captain Jack, Dick the Fish, N Mac, Mr X, Tom the Fiddler, Benny Cheese, Daniel Jones and, of course, Dylan Thomas. Come think of it, the list seems a bit like the cast of *Under Milk Wood*!

There are many other lost taverns for which space has prevented inclusion. Among these are the Albion, Butchers' Arms, Commercial, Foresters' Arms, Greyhound, Rose and Crown, and Shi Aground at Mumbles; Red Cow at Bishopston; Penrice Arms at Nicholaston; Cefn Bryn Inn at Hillend; Farmers Arms at Llanddewi; Hope and Anchor and New Inn at Iscoed; and the Collier Arms at Wernffrwd. There is also anecdotal evidence of the Flying Fish at Wernffrwd and numer others, including the Albert Inn in Mumbles.

I suppose it is not surprising that I have written a book about pubs – my father was a landlo and I lived and worked in the pub. I'm also a member of the Campaign for Real Ale (CAMRA My research has been carried out in between many other hobbies, including walking and travell and singing with the Morriston Orpheus Choir. I've found it a fascinating journey – I hope yo do too!

Brian E. Da
January 2

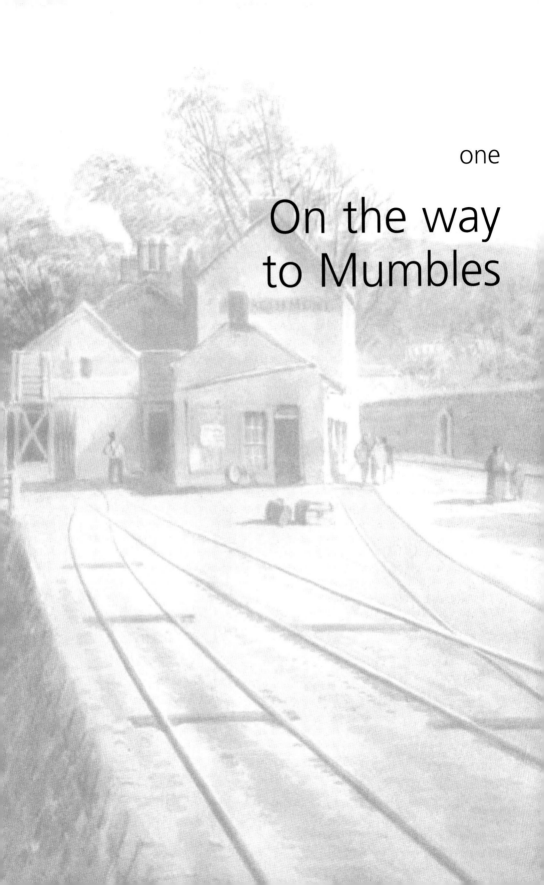

one

On the way to Mumbles

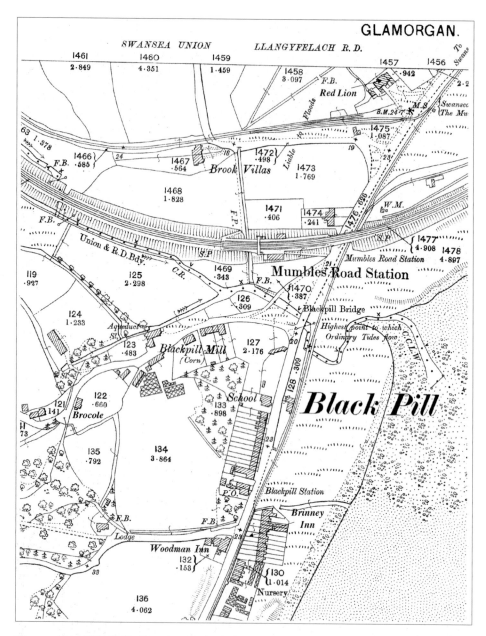

The map shows Blackpill village in 1898 with the locations of four pubs that served the village over the centuries. The Red Lion is at the top, where the Clyne Valley tramway branches off the old Mumbles Railway. The tramway serviced coal mining, iron and timber industries in the Clyne Valley. Near Blackpill Mill was another pub, at a house called Brocole. This alehouse possibly dates back to the 1750s, when Henry Morgan was the innkeeper and miller. In the early nineteenth century there was a chemical works in the valley which produced arsenic, and the pub was used by its workers. It must also have been frequented by farmers visiting the mill and may have been called the Farmers Arms (recorded in the vicinity in the 1840s). The Brinney Inn existed in the first half of the nineteenth century but was demolished and the terrace of houses was built. The Woodman Inn replaced it and survives today.

This Thomas Baxter sketch of 1818 shows the Red Lion with a coal wagon on the tramway. In the 1820s, Lewis Weston Dillwyn, the distinguished Swansea scientist, 'went to tea' at the inn, also called the Halfway House because of its position between Swansea and Mumbles. In 1855, Abel Vivian became the licensee and in 1860 he revived the Blackpill Races. In 1869, the inn's alehouse licence was refused and occupier Samuel Jones carried on business as a coal merchant – but his wife, Mary, apparently continued brewing beer!

The Halfway House continued as a brewery and beer retailer and in 1900 the licence transferred to Thomas Griffiths, another coal merchant, who was 'Licensed to sell Beer and Cider to be consumed Off the Premises'. The off-licence closed in 1925 and the house was later demolished. The Halfway Garage is now at the site – I wonder how many people filling up their cars know that the old pub was once there dispensing liquid of a much more palatable kind!

Mrs Elizabeth Fitt was landlady of the Woodman between 1924 and 1932. The pub was opened in its present location in 1859 after moving across the road – the Brinney Inn was renamed the Woodman about ten years earlier. John John was licensee at both locations and was the original woodman, later becoming an oyster-dredger. His son, Thomas, was a tram-man who drove the horse cars which preceded the steam trains on the Mumbles Railway. During Mrs Fitt's time the electric trams started running. The Woodman was in a prominent position, with the railway waiting room alongside. Bishopston farmers changed horses there on their way to Swansea market. The stables were also used as a makeshift mortuary for anyone found washed up on the beach, and for one unfortunate woman whose mangled corpse was found on the railway one evening in 1890.

The Woodman was sold to Evans Bevan Vale of Neath Brewery in 1954. The picture shows the Clyne Bar at the rear, which replaced the old stables.

Right: Edith Cousens, with her husband and daughter. Edith became landlady of the Woodman in 1916, following her mother, Sarah Maddams. Edith's father, George Maddams, was a celebrated figure serving in Her Majesty's Treasury at Whitehall. He was a messenger attached to the Prime Minister's residence and, on one occasion, had just announced the arrival of Lord Iddesleigh to Lord Salisbury, when Iddesleigh collapsed into his arms and died. George Maddams himself died at the Woodman in 1899.

Below: The 'knocking down ceremony' of a huge pile of pennies collected for Swansea Blind at the Woodman, *c.* 1980. The picture includes long-term licensees Gwyneth and Cyril John (third and fourth from the left). Cyril was a popular landlord and well-known sportsman, being a former professional footballer and boxing champion. He also served in Burma in the Second World War and was a Japanese prisoner of war.

The Currant Tree at West Cross, sketched here in 1878, was an ancient inn reputed to be a smugglers' haunt. In 1845, a burglary took place when some silver was taken by 'someone acquainted with the premises' and in 1893, landlady Mrs Hopkins died after being hit by a customer! The inn was the first past the three-mile limit from Swansea and, unsurprisingly, was very popular on Sundays. The pub burned down in 1896, being replaced by the West Cross Hotel alongside.

Sunday visitors continued to flock to the rebuilt West Cross Hotel but strong objections were raised in the early 1900s when large numbers of drunken people from the train were reported behaving in a 'disorderly and uproarious' manner. However, the licence was retained and gradually it became more respectable, although the landlord was convicted of stealing potatoes in 1917! This aerial view dates from the 1960s – the houses on the left have since been demolished.

Advertisement for the Linden Tree, from a 1972 holiday guide. The purpose-built estate pub was opened by Hancocks in 1967; its first manager was Major Charles Durrant. Although modern, the pub has its stories. One of the locals once rode a horse into the bar, and it's rumoured to be haunted by the ghost of an old cellar man!

The 'Sunday Club' at the Linden Tree Hotel, 1983. The group mainly consisted of local ex-servicemen. From left to right: Trevor ? (ex-RAF), Haydn Randall (ex-Tank Corps who served in the desert), Harry ? (ex-Welsh Guards), Aubrey Habberfield (ex-Commando, took part in the Normandy landings), Bill Coleman (ex-Royal Artillery, served in North Africa and Italy), Peter Shenton (Welch Regiment, who lost his leg after being wounded in Normandy), and Dewi Pritchard, who was an engineering student during the war, later on reserve.

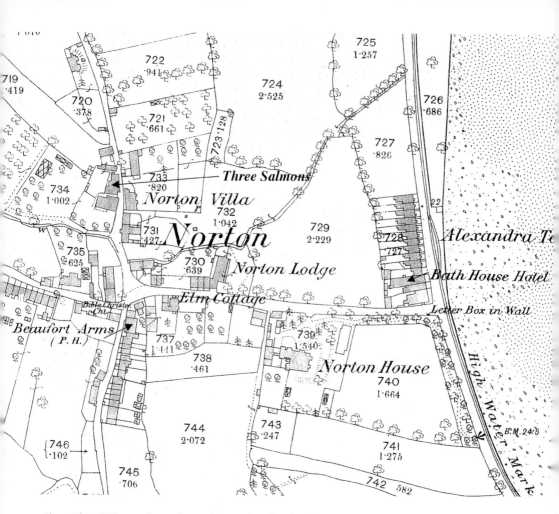

The map shows the following labels and plot numbers:

719 ·419, 720 ·378, 721 ·661, 722 ·941, 723 ·128, 724 2·525, 725 1·257, 726 ·686, 727 ·826, 728 ·727, 729 2·229, 730 ·639, 731 ·427, 732 1·042, 733 ·820, 734 1·002, 735 ·625, 737 1·411, 738 ·461, 739 1·540, 740 1·664, 741 1·275, 742 582, 743 ·247, 744 2·072, 745 ·706, 746 ·102

Three Salmons — Norton Villa — Norton — Norton Lodge — Elm Cottage — Bible Christian Chapel — Beaufort Arms (P.H.) — Alexandra T. — Bath House Hotel — Letter Box in Wall — Norton House — High Water Mark — B.M. 24·5

Above: This 1877 map shows three of Norton's pubs: the Three Salmons, the Beaufort Arms and the Bath House Hotel. Other pubs recorded at Norton in the nineteenth century were the Dove, the Cross Inn and the Wheatsheaf. The Three Salmons was in business between 1827 and 1856 when Mary Jenkins and her daughter (also Mary) ran the beerhouse, and were also laundresses. The old building stood long after its days as a pub and was demolished around 1980. The Bath House closed as a pub in the 1890s, but the Beaufort Arms is still going strong.

Opposite above: Delivering to the Bath House 'Family Hotel' in the 1890s. The Bath House was built in 1855, and an alehouse licence was granted to Charles Fuller in 1865. In 1869, Miss Jones was advertising board and lodging at £1 per week. In 1888, a local man was summoned for not being a bona fide traveller – he was found sitting in the kitchen with a pint of beer – he lived within a mile but pretended he'd come from Swansea. He was fined 15s or ten days. The following year, Mr Slocombe of Boar's Pit Farm gave a dinner at the hotel for the large number of persons who bought manure from him! The pub lasted until the mid-1890s, and a temperance hotel stood on the corner in 1896. Today, the premises include the Tidesreach Guest House.

Opposite below: An advertisement from the *Bristol Mercury Guide to the Mumbles*, from 1884.

The Beaufort Arms, Norton, when William Williams was licensee (1925-32). The lean-to shop was later incorporated and is now the pub cellar. The pub was named The Ship on the Beaufort Estate map of 1802 and was offered for sale in 1837, becoming the Beaufort Arms soon afterwards. In 1859, the Oystermouth Castle Lodge of Oddfellows was set up there and host James Brayley laid on a sumptuous repast. By 1903 the house was 'not fit for a public house, with small and low rooms and in a dilapidated and filthy condition' but was granted a six-day licence provided things were improved – it was then renovated. Hancocks leased the house in 1935, and their annual trade in 1937 was 195½ barrels of beer and 256 gallons of wine and spirits. In 1940, ladies toilets were provided and the bar and rear smoking room were later converted into one large bar. The Beaufort continues at the centre of village life as it has done for over 200 years.

Opposite above: The Beaufort darts team celebration dinner after they won the championship in 1954. Reg Cottle, a well-known Mumbles character, is marked with an 'X' here because he appeared so frequently in the *Mumbles News* that everybody knew him – thus acquiring the nickname 'Mr X'! Darts has always been popular at the Beaufort, as has the card game Euchre.

Opposite below: The famous Mumbles Raft Race has been held annually since 1984 to raise funds for the Mumbles Lifeboat. Thousands turn out for the event and many local organisations and pubs build rafts. This magnificent construction replicating the Beaufort pub was launched for the 1997 race. Intrepid sailors are, from left to right: Byron Gates, Vicky Passmore, Sue Bryant, Jill Evans, Scottie Adams, Rita Carlsen, Becky John and Tony Carlsen.

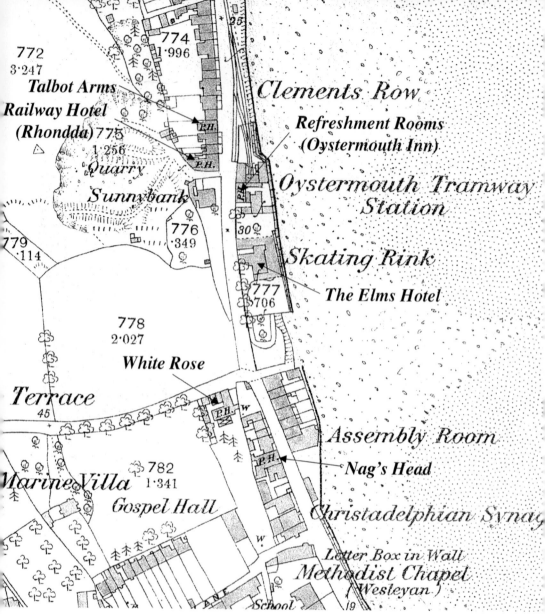

This map shows Oystermouth tramway station in 1877, with its cluster of public houses awaiting thirsty visitors. The railway reopened to passenger traffic in 1860, and in 1877 steam was introduced to compete with the horse-drawn trams. Thousands travelled from Swansea on Sundays, taking advantage of the three-mile rule. The majority of these were not bona fide travellers, but were exploiting the rule in an attempt to get intoxicated in Mumbles. Indignant locals called them 'bona-fide humbugs'. In the 1880s, there were many reports of the 'lower classes' brawling and swearing, with 'drunkenness scandalously prevalent, especially among young girls, who seemed to cause most of the fights'! The mayhem reached its peak just before the last train left. The railway was extended to the new pier in 1898, bringing even more visitors and, in the early 1900s, the temperance movement campaigned fervently to close down some of the rougher Mumbles pubs. Licence renewals were objected to on a routine basis and three of the pubs were closed in that period – the Talbot, Rhondda and Oystermouth Inns. The White Rose and Nag's Head survived and a century later they still stand at the start of the celebrated Mumbles Mile.

A painting of Oystermouth tramway station in 1883, by Alfred Parkman. The Refreshment Rooms are adjoining, with The Elms behind (with the chimneys). The Railway Hotel (Rhondda) is on the far right. The Elms Hotel was licensed in 1856, but despite being a 'superior hotel' it lasted for just ten years before reverting to a private house. A roller-skating rink was in full swing there in the 1870s and the house survived well into the twentieth century. The Refreshment Rooms was first licensed in 1867 when Abel Vivian arrived from the Red Lion in Blackpill. The Vivians also ran a livery stables with conveyances to the bays, wagonettes, and hearses for funerals. A ballad of 1877 by Frank Richards paints the picture:

By the Oystermouth tram
There's such a tight jam
Each t'other one jostles and jumbles
But at last he's put down
As you enter the town
Close to Vivian's Hotel at the Mumbles.

The Vivians kept the Refreshment Rooms, later called the Oystermouth Inn, until 1902. The pub soon suffered licensing objections and even though the house was well-run, with 'a better class of customer than the Talbot', the licence was refused in 1907. The house and yard later became Mumbles Dairy, and the site was cleared in the 1960s to become the dairy car park.

The Rhondda Hotel in 1906. Originally licensed in 1861 as the Oystermouth Railway Hotel, its name changed in 1899, reflecting the rail extension to the Pier by the Rhondda & Swansea Bay Railway. Visitors from the Rhondda Valleys would have felt welcome! Caroline Williams was landlady in its final days – it closed in 1908. By then it was 'a very old house in a bad state' with 'customers of the poorest kind and lowest class'. It became two cottages, one has since been demolished.

The Rhondda Hotel was on the left of this row, with the Talbot Arms fourth along. The Talbot was in business by 1841 and attracted the 'travellers'. In 1889, one such was fined for being drunk – he said he went down to Mumbles for a mouthful of fresh air. The Bench said he'd mixed the air with too much whisky! The Talbot's licence was opposed because it was structurally unsuitable with poor sanitary arrangements, and it closed in 1907.

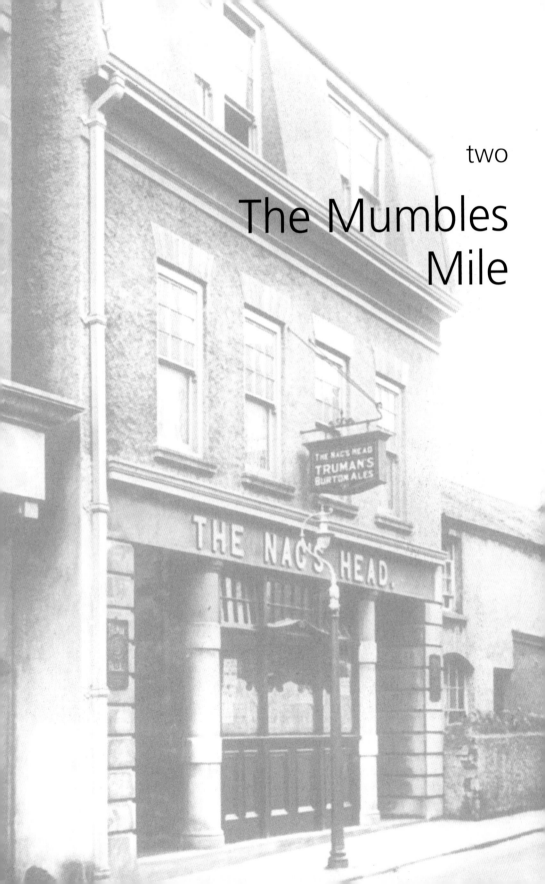

two

The Mumbles Mile

John Williams established the White Rose at The Dunns in 1856, having been refused a spirit licence at an earlier location in Clements Row. This photograph comes from the 'dawn of photography' in the 1850s and was taken by Mary Dillwyn from Oystermouth Castle. 'Williams's White Rose' can just be seen on the front of the house.

The pub was extended and two shops were added. Richard Hobbs took over in 1877 and this picture probably shows Richard and wife Mary outside the doorway. Mary continued as licensee until 1906, and was described as 'an exemplary landlady'. At that time, the house was 'kept very clean' and had a stable for four horses. Although it was referred to the Compensation Authority for closure, it managed to hold onto its licence.

This sketch of Mumbles before the railway was extended shows the White Rose Inn. In 1907, the pub had a ground-floor bar, and a smoking room 'unlighted from outside with a dark kitchen behind, down some steps'. It was considered structurally unfit for visitors and shortly afterwards the pub was substantially rebuilt and the mock-Tudor style first appeared. The rebuilt pub was sold in 1912 for £2,425.

The White Rose in 1998, much altered from the old nineteenth-century alehouse. In 1984 a major expansion took in the premises on the corner of The Dunns at a cost of £75,000. The doorway that Richard Hobbs stood outside a hundred years earlier still remains. The White Rose is considered to be the start of the famous (or infamous) Mumbles Mile pub crawl.

The Dunns, Mumbles, with the Nag's Head on the right with a lamp above the door, *c.* 1922. The shops on the left were demolished in 1971 to widen the road. The Nag's Head is over 200 years old and was probably named after the livery stables alongside. The Methodists apparently held meetings there in 1795 – their opinion of the place was very different 100 years later! In 1806, landlord Jenkin Jenkins was criticised for inhumanely refusing to take in the mortally wounded William Locke, master of the sloop *Delight*, who'd fallen from the shrouds during a gale in the bay. Ironically, Jenkins' grandson became the first coxswain of the Mumbles Lifeboat, and two of his great-grandsons died heroically in the Mumbles Lifeboat disaster of 1883. Daniel Taylor was innkeeper of the Nag's Head during the first half of the nineteenth century, followed by Edwin Peachey, who married Taylor's daughter. Peachey also ran the livery stables. In 1890, licensee Frederick Griffin was summoned for keeping a disorderly house – two women of ill fame who'd arrived on the tram were found by PC David in a back room with a number of men. Needless to say this was on a Sunday. In the early 1900s, temperance campaigners objected, saying that trade on Sundays was 'working class, rather low, from the train', drunkenness and bad language was rife, the house was dark with rooms requiring gaslight in daytime, and was in a narrow part where carts couldn't stop without obstructing.

Right: The Nag's Head survived the licence objections and was later rebuilt and a third storey added, as shown in this picture from around the 1930s. In 1955 it was said to be a real students' pub, where licensees Ernest and Jennie John went out of their way to make students welcome, taking a paternal pride in 'their boys.' There was always a sing-song on a Saturday night or before a big dance.

Below: Mr and Mrs Fred Bowden, licensees of the Nag's Head between 1963 and 1983. The pub was renamed the Oystercatcher in 1972, before changing back to the Nag's Head in 1995. Over the years the small rooms were merged to become the present open-plan arrangement – very different from the old tavern of the 1790s.

The shoreline and oyster boats outside the Marine Hotel, *c.* 1890. The hotel, now known as the Village Inn, dates back to 1734 when Phillip Powell was granted a lease for Horsepool House. It was then right on the seashore near the Horsepool, the sea-inlet and oyster skiff lay-up. By 1844 it was named the New Inn and the landlord, Herbert Lloyd, was a master mariner and oyster dealer. In 1877, when Thomas Honey was landlord, a famous character named Hobart Pasha, honorary commander of the Turkish fleet, was resident. Mrs Honey was pregnant at the time and it was decided that if the baby was a boy and born before Hobart's ship left the bay, they would name the baby after him. This duly happened and the baby was named Hobart Pasha Honey! In due time, Hobart himself had a son who was given the same name. The old building was rebuilt and the name was changed to the Marine Hotel in 1888. Around this time, the Courts Leet met at the Marine, and the ancient appointments were made, including that of honorary ale taster. The hotel was described as a splendid house, with good stabling and coach house, but in 1906 a man left his horse and trap outside, and during his absence two young men got in the trap and drove off!

Above: The Marine Hotel in the 1920s. In the early 1930s the Marine was one of Dylan Thomas's first calls when he visited Mumbles, which he described as 'a rather nice village despite its name, right on the edge of the sea'.

Right: The Marine's name changed to La Parisienne in the 1970s, and later became Hudsons and then Vincent's in the 1990s. Spanish landlord, Vincent Moreno, was well known for his tapas and greeted numerous famous visitors, including Prince Albert of Monaco, Lord Archer and Kingsley Amis. The name changed to the Village Inn in 2000.

ALWAYS A
FRIENDLY WELCOME
AT THE

LA PARISIENNE

MUMBLES, SWANSEA

ENTERTAINMENT
EVERY EVENING

FULLY LICENSED

Mr. & Mrs.
David Thomas
Telephone: 66339

The Waterloo Stores, around the turn of the century. Previously a mariner's house, the Waterloo's first licence was granted to George Bradford in 1862. The Bradford family also ran the Waterloo Hotel and bonded stores in Swansea. The house was a bottling, wine and spirit stores, with a public house on-licence. An inquest was held there in 1869 after fourteen-year-old Martha Colston, daughter of Revd Colston of Thistleboon House, sadly drowned while bathing at Rotherslade Bay. In 1890, the landlord, Charles Gelderd, was summoned for serving a local man on a Sunday; William Jenkins, an elderly Mumbles man, was seen by PC David to cross the promenade, look up and down, and then run to the Waterloo Stores and into the Bottle and Jug department, bolting the door after him. The policeman ran to the door and saw Jenkins at the bar, with the defendant bringing him a 'blue' (an old measure, between a half and a pint) or a pint of beer, he was unable to say which. The defendant said he had given him a glass of waste! Both were fined by the Bench. In 1929 the pub was purchased by Hancock's Brewery, and in 1931 the name was changed to the Waterloo Hotel.

Above: The *Mumbles News* of March 1976 pictured landlord Terry Thomas, who had recently taken over the Waterloo Hotel. The picture includes his friend Ed Pressdee.

Right: An advertisement for the Waterloo Hotel from 1981. Vincent Moreno was mine host of the Waterloo for ten years before moving on to Vincent's. In 1983, while laughter was still echoing around the bar of the Waterloo about Captain Jack's mishap in Ilfracombe when he missed the boat back to Mumbles, Senor Moreno went on a trip with a local yachtsman in his speedboat. When they got to Pwlldu, the boat ran out of petrol and they had to be towed back to Mumbles. Last laugh to Captain Jack! In the late 1980s, the pub name changed to the William Hancock, recalling the old brewery. In recent times, the pub has been the Welsh headquarters of the Monster Raving Loony Party.

YOUR NEW HOST
VINCENT MORENO
Welcomes you to the
"Waterloo"
Southend — Mumbles

A "BASS" HOUSE

Above: The white building with two chimneys in the centre foreground of this view is the old Fountain Inn, *c.* 1880s. The inn was doing business in the early nineteenth century, and by 1838 Richard and Eleanor Thomas were licensees. They lived at the Fountain with their eleven children. In 1858 Richard was charged with opening on Sunday before the termination of divine service. He was fined sixpence plus costs. The inn closed in 1869 and one of Richard's sons, John, later lived there with his family.

Left: John and Frances Thomas, who lived at the old Fountain Inn. John was a mariner who served in the Crimean War and was an oyster merchant with a few skiffs. The old inn was demolished in around 1890, making way for the promenade gardens. Mumbles poet 'American' Jones wrote:

Johnny Thomas was a funny old shade,
He knocked down his house to make the promenade.

John Thomas was the grandfather of well-known Mumbles character 'Puss' Thomas.

The Antelope Inn (left), on the corner of Village Lane, around the 1880s. The old building that became the pub is at the rear and was extended sideways and then outwards. It was called the Oystermouth Castle Hotel when John Ackland obtained a new licence in 1867. The pub was renamed the Antelope three years later by David Rees, who previously kept the Antelope in Swansea – he clearly brought the name with him. In 1888, landlord Henry James was summoned for opening on Sunday and supplying a pint of rum to Edmund Bevan, a seaman, who later assaulted Police Sergeant Howells. Although the case was dismissed, the rum was confiscated! The licence was objected to in 1907 because of the inn's disorderly character and riotous conduct – it was a Buckley's house at the time. It was described as a poor house, peculiarly constructed, with a stable with three stalls for two horses each. It managed to keep its licence.

The Antelope Hotel in the 1950s, when Timothy Perkins took over. Tim transformed the décor and steered the pub away from its disreputable past. He built up a new clientele and attracted the literati of Swansea, serving Pimms with 'half of Swansea Market's fruit stall in the glass!' Anthony Hopkins, Wilfred Bramble (Steptoe), Wynford Vaughan Thomas, Garfield Sobers, Ryan Davies, Michael Heseltine, Kenneth Williams, Emlyn Williams, Tom Bell, Kingsley Amis and Vernon Watkins were some of the visitors. Dylan Thomas visited in the 1930s and '50s, seeing both aspects of the Antelope – I wonder which he preferred?

The traditional Watneys dray, delivering to Mumbles in 1978, calls in at the Antelope Inn. Licensees Betty and Graham Davies and Beryl Hill are on the left.

Dylan Thomas and Mumbles

'Oh woe, woe, woe unto Mumbles and the oystered beer', wrote Dylan Thomas in 1932 after a drinking session in Mumbles with his friend Daniel Jones. Dylan's association with Mumbles began as a child with visits to his Aunt Dosie in Newton – he called Mumbles the place 'where the aunties grew'! He liked travelling on the Mumbles train, 'rattling along to a beery and fleshly Oystermouth', and visiting 'the gaunt pier with its skeleton legs'. Dylan left school in 1931 to work as a reporter and joined the Swansea Little Theatre, a group of players based at Mumbles, between 1931 and 1934. Between rehearsals he frequented the Mumbles pubs, including the Antelope and Mermaid, 'communing with these two legendary creatures'. Later in his life, Dylan returned to Mumbles and would sometimes visit the Antelope. Apparently, he sat in front of the fire scribbling, but the landlady used to throw any writings left behind onto the fire! His famous work, *Under Milk Wood*, is grounded in the Welsh seaside locations Dylan visited and lived in – some of the inhabitants of Llareggub have uncanny similarities to real-life Mumbles characters! It was on a trip to Gower, during his time as a Mumbles actor, that Dylan shouted 'they are rejecting me now, but the day will come when the name of Dylan Thomas will be echoed from shore to shore. Only I won't be alive to hear it'. Prophetic words indeed.

The Dylan Thomas Society of Wales was formed in the late 1970s. Its founder chairman was former Antelope landlord Timothy Perkins, a Little Theatre player and acquaintance of Dylan. This rehearsal at the Antelope, seen here around 1977, features, from left to right: Valerie Davies, John Rhys Thomas, Megan Evans, Dudley Evans and Timothy Perkins.

Above: Oyster boats on the shingle, with the Prince of Wales and Antelope behind, *c.* 1880. The Ship Inn stood on the site of the Prince of Wales in the early 1800s and was a pretty rough place. In 1844, landlord John Hoskin, his wife and daughter were charged with assaulting Elizabeth Morgan. Elizabeth had gone to the Ship to get her husband to return home. Some 'high words took place' and Hoskin struck her before his wife and daughter joined in! The husband was probably too drunk to care. The magistrate convicted Hoskin and fined him 20s, cautioning him about the disorderly character of the house. The pub name changed when it was re-licensed in 1862, probably celebrating the pending Royal wedding. The Howells family ran the pub at that time and were mariners and oyster dealers. The pub was frequented by oyster fishermen and was rebuilt in the 1870s, at the height of the oyster boom.

Opposite above: The Prince of Wales in the 1880s after the rebuild – the earlier pub was probably similar to the ruined cottages alongside. In 1883 the pub was obtained by Fultons, the Swansea wine and spirits merchants, who owned it until the 1960s. Benny Cheese, 'a real character', managed the hotel for many years in the early 1900s. He was reputed to have the finest cellar in Mumbles (although the cellar used to flood at high tide!). 'Cheese's' was one of Dylan Thomas's regular haunts in the 1930s.

In 1968, Edith McDonald (better known as Mrs Mac) retired from the Prince of Wales, having arrived there during the Second World War. Immensely popular with her customers, it was a sad day when this lady last called 'time'. In the 1980s and '90s the pub became known as Monroes and later Waltzers when fairground waltzers were dotted around the bar! The old pub gradually became run down and was acquired by Patrick's restaurant in 2001.

The Horse's Head, or *Mari Lwyd*, custom dates from ancient times and is celebrated at Christmas. The Mumbles Horse's Head story dates from the 1870s, when the skull of an old Gower horse, 'Sharper', was dug up at Barland and reburied in Limeslade. The 'clean' skull was then dug up again and the jaws wired together, with a broom handle to hold it upright. It was decorated with ribbons and rosettes, with green glass bottle bottoms for eyes and a sheet for a man to hide under. The Horse's Head was first paraded around the village by William Jenkins, his brothers and friends, who sang special songs, including 'Poor Old Horse'. Sharper's jaws would be opened and people would 'feed' him fruit and mince pies (with ale for the revellers). Although the custom ceased during the war years, it has been revived many times since. The picture shows the Horse's Head at the Prince of Wales, Christmas 1947, carried by 'Holy Joe' Michael with supporters Len 'Yank' Jones, Evan Jones, George Baglow, Sid Bale, Jack Jenkins, Joe Winstone, Charle Davies (Sully), Tom Davies (Russe). The head has remained with the same family throughout its existence, and in recent years Bill and Len Bowden have continued the tradition, helping to raise substantial funds for charity.

Right: Captain George Phillips, landlord of the Ship and Castle Hotel from around 1814 until his death in 1860. He was a master mariner and oyster boat owner, and leased limestone quarries in Mumbles. The hotel was built in 1737 and George's mother, Rachel Phillips, was licensee before him. After George's death his daughters took over. In 1843 one of George's oyster boats sank with the loss of four lives, and it was suggested they either had 'too much sail' or the men had a cask of beer on board and were intoxicated! No blame was attributed to Captain Phillips.

Below: The Ship and Castle Hotel, with the Mermaid Hotel in the background, *c.* 1890. In the 1850s, Royal Mail omnibuses ran from Swansea to the Ship and Castle, which was well known for the quality of its accommodation. In residence in 1881 was a visitor named Tudor James, described in the census for that year as 'half clergyman, half imbecile'! The Ship and Castle burned down in the 1890s and was completely rebuilt. Afterwards, it was described as 'up-to-date, one of the best houses in Mumbles, with fine stables where carriages could be placed'.

The Ship and Castle Hotel

The MUMBLES,
Near SWANSEA.

Replete with every comfort. Pleasantly situated, overlooking the Sea and Swansea Bay.

Nicely furnished Billiard, Coffee and Smoke Rooms.

MODERATE TARIFF.

Special Terms for Week-end Visitors.

For particulars apply to Miss I. BATES.

An early photograph of the Mermaid Hotel, *c.* 1853. At the time of the Napoleonic Wars, the hotel was the known as the 'New Mermaid' (the 'Old Mermaid' was further along the front). Jane Stephens was the landlady – her husband John was a mariner who drowned in 1791, and her son Benjamin died in captivity in France after eight years incarceration. In 1821 a visitor wrote in his diary of his ride on the railway to Mumbles and his friendly reception at the New Mermaid Inn from Mrs Stephens, 'a jolly looking woman, extremely fat'! In 1832, a meeting was held at the Mermaid which eventually led to the establishment of the famous Mumbles Lifeboat. In 1843 the hotel's roof was blown off in a gale and Captain Stephens was praised for saving his family and the house from destruction.

Opposite: This 1903 advertisement shows the rebuilt Ship and Castle Hotel. Unfortunately, by the 1920s, its standards had declined drastically. The police raided the place in the early hours of Sunday 3 April 1927, finding the premises being used as a disorderly house (brothel). The landlord and his wife were heavily fined and their licence was forfeited forever. The Ship and Castle in nearby Newton was forced to change its name to the Newton Inn because would-be customers went there instead! The hotel became the 'men only' Conservative Club. The club remains today – the veranda and balcony have gone but the building is largely unchanged.

In 1860 the Mermaid was described as 'a superior hotel, respectable and well conducted, catering for the numerous visitors flocking to Mumbles'. On 10 March 1863 Mumbles celebrated the Royal wedding of the Prince of Wales. Houses and boats were decorated with bunting, and a dinner for the poor was held with the sumptuous fare provided by Mr Knight of the Mermaid. In 1880 the Mermaid was described as 'a quaint old place, with flower-veiled front and arboured garden reaching down to shingle at the water's edge'.

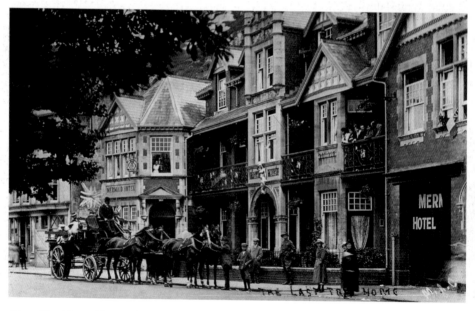

Above: The Mermaid was rebuilt in 1898, and the new hotel opened at the same time as the Mumbles Pier. The picture shows a carriage and four ready for 'the last trip home' to Swansea. The Mermaid was a magnificent hotel in the Edwardian period, with splendid rooms commanding views over Swansea Bay.

During the 1950s, the Mermaid's landlord was Richard Williams, popularly known as 'Dick the Fish'. He was a larger-than-life character, a big man with a big moustache and a vintage Bentley parked in the old stables. One night, Dick returned to the Mermaid after a boozy night out with friends, inviting them in for a nightcap. There was an appetizing smell coming from the kitchen where they found a huge 'stew' on the cooker. They tucked in, washing it down with a couple of pints. Next morning, Dick's wife, Enid, asked the hungover Dick what had happened to the scraps she'd been boiling up for the dogs – they'd eaten it all!

The Mermaid Hotel's licence expired in 1992. Sadly, the following year, the building was damaged by three fires. The picture shows the Mermaid boarded up after the fires, awaiting demolition. It was pulled down in 1996, and in 2002 the site was redeveloped. The new 'Mermaid's Retreat' includes seafront apartments and a smart restaurant.

Above: The Beaufort Arms, Mumbles, originally known as the Old Mermaid, dates back to the 1700s. In 1805 it was offered for let as 'an old and well-accustomed public house, with a large brewhouse and a good copper'. It was renamed the Beaufort Arms by 1837 and offered for sale by the Beaufort Estate. It was then owned by the Bennett family, who were also farmers and oyster skiff owners. By the early 1900s it was leased by Swansea United Brewery and frequented by the 'rougher classes', especially on Sundays, when its 'doors were wide open' and thousands of excursionists were visiting Mumbles on the railway. It inevitably had convictions for permitting drunkenness (and even for serving lifeboat men on their return!) The Justices were under pressure to close troublesome Mumbles pubs and the Beaufort was referred to the Compensation Authority and closed in 1920. The pub buildings still exist as a sailmaker's premises and are probably among the oldest in Mumbles. Remnants of old cottages still exist at the rear, with an old well in the corner. The old brewhouse is now a flat with a sail-loft above.

Opposite above: The George Hotel in Victorian times. In 1803 it had been called the George and Dragon, no doubt providing refreshment for man and beast. A number of landlords in the nineteenth century were sailors, and Yacht Club meetings were held there. Frederick Birks, landlord in the 1870s, was a boat owner who entered the Regattas. He also complained in the *Cambrian* that dead bodies found on the beach were kept in his stables! In 1887, a fire destroyed the bar and the landlady's son, James Brown, heroically helped people to escape.

Troops outside the George and Beaufort during the First World War. Between 1912 and 1950 John Noel and his then wife, Catherine, were licensees. Their son, William Noel, tragically died in the 1947 Mumbles Lifeboat disaster, when the crew of eight were killed at Sker Point trying to save the *Samtampa*, whose crew of thirty-nine also perished.

Following the Second World War, a 'sea of people' from the train would visit the George, where someone often played the piano and people sang in Welsh. Many alterations were made in the 1950s and '60s to improve the hotel, and Evans Bevan Vale of Neath Brewery took it over. Whitbread later acquired the George and converted it into a Beefeater Steak House, pictured here in 1986. Brains Brewery converted it into a bar and restaurant called Salt in 2004.

Mumbles beach, with the Pilot Inn in the background next to the Temperance Hotel, in the 1880s. The Pilot was first licensed in 1849, when Samuel Ace, mariner and pilot, opened the inn. He'd previously kept the Talbot Arms in Clements Row. In 1862, an inquest was held for James Smith, who had died near the Pilot Inn. The jury returned a verdict of 'Died by Visitation of God'. In the 1870s and '80s Captain Henry Mills, a Scotsman and former shipmaster at the Port of Swansea, was landlord. At this time, the Pilot was a popular haunt for mariners, fishermen and oyster dredgers. The inn's close proximity to the shore made it an ideal spot from which to view the Mumbles Regattas, at which vast crowds gathered.

Opposite below: The Ostreme Parade of 1975. The parade terminated at the George Hotel, where the Mayor and Mayoress of Swansea greeted participants and had afternoon tea at the hotel. These pageants were arranged in the early 1970s to raise funds for the new Ostreme Community Hall in Mumbles.

Above: A charabanc outing for the Pilot's regulars in 1924. The Pilot survived the licence objections of 1904, despite a number of convictions, and served bread and cheese and oysters to its many Sunday visitors. In 1914, licensee John Paine volunteered to fight in the First World War and was accepted at sixty-four years of age! He was an ex-policeman who previously kept the Plough and Harrow in Murton.

Left: The Pilot Inn in the early 1930s, when Tom Newbury was landlord. The Southend Temperance Hotel is alongside. The Pilot was much used by yachtsmen and Mumbles Yacht Club was formed there in 1938. The exterior hasn't changed much, but the old public bar, snug and kitchen were merged into one large saloon bar in 1967. Despite many changes and the passage of time, the Pilot has always retained its maritime connections.

Mumbles Pier, hotel and station, *c.* 1910. The pier opened in 1898 and became a very popular place of recreation where grand shows were held. Thousands of visitors arrived on the train and there were regular steamer departures from the pier to Ilfracombe, Devon, and other destinations. Bank Holidays were particularly hectic and in 1906 a seaman was fined for assaulting the piermaster, Captain Twomey, who was attempting to throw him out of the second-class bar due to his rowdy behaviour.

The Pier Hotel buildings, with the adjoining Winter Gardens pavilion, in 1911. The pavilion held around 1,000 people and was well packed, especially for Sunday concerts (admission 1s). Artistes taking part over the years included Covent Garden opera singers, choirs and military bands, including the Grenadier Guards and the Morriston Choir conducted by Ivor Sims.

In 1937 the Amusement Equipment Co. took over the operation of the pier, and Hancocks Brewery leased the Pier Hotel. Hancocks retained the hotel until 1950 when AEC took it over and also rebuilt the pier. The two doorways on the left are the present-day Salty and Toby Bars. Sadly, the Mumbles Railway closed in 1960, despite opposition including a petition to the House of Lords by the pier owners. The railway closure has been much lamented but the pier and hotel have continued to prosper.

In 1998 the pier's centenary was celebrated. To mark the occasion, the Mumbles Beer Festival launched a Pierhead Special Ale and pier owner Stan Bollom pulled the first pint. Here, festival organisers celebrate the occasion with Stan Bollom (left) and Will Fleming of Brains Brewery, the festival sponsors.

three

From
back streets
to bays

TO BE LET, in the Mumbles,

AND MAY BE ENTERED UPON IMMEDIATELY,

THE well known FREE PUBLIC HOUSE called "THE PARK INN." It is well adapted for Grocery Business, or both. A good Brewhouse and Cellar with plentiful supply of water. Rent moderate.

For further particulars apply to Mr. John Woollacott Newton, Oystermouth.

Above: Park Street in Mumbles dates from the early 1850s and this advertisement for the Park Inn appeared in the *Cambrian* on 19 December 1862. Charles Davies, a mariner and oyster dredger, was granted the new licence in 1863. In 1870, Charles' brother, James, was found drunkenly knocking on the door of the Park Inn by PC Letherin. He was cursing and swearing, and challenging his brother to come out and fight. He was fined £2 or fourteen days. At that time, the pub had eight rooms, a brewhouse and a blacksmith's shop at the back. In 1887, landlord Alfred Pyne was summoned for 'impeding the Tramway Company's officials'. He went to Mumbles Station and attempted to roll away a cask of beer without paying 6d carriage. A scuffle with the stationmaster ensued and Pyne received two black eyes! He was found not guilty.

Left: Crowhurst's Brewery leased the Park Inn by 1880 and in 1890 became part of Swansea United Breweries, which Trumans took over in 1926. This picture dates from the early 1930s.

Above: Ronnie and Winnie Jenkins ran the Park Inn between 1932 and 1970. In this 1960s photogtraph, they show off one of Winn's works of art to regulars, including Mr X (right) and 'Captain Jack' Williams. There's a story about one regular who sat in the corner of the bar. He used the same seat for years and if anyone else sat there he made them move. After he died, someone else sat in his spot and was warned that the previous occupant might be watching! He brushed it off as a joke, whereupon a plate fell from the wall and hit him on the head!

Right: In recent years Park Street has regularly won Mumbles in Bloom awards and the Park Inn has been popular for its real ales, winning Swansea CAMRA's Pub of the Year award twice. The seeds of Mumbles Beer Festival were sown there in the 1990s.

T. Bevan.

In the mid-1990s, a group of Mumbles real ale enthusiasts formed MADRAS (Mumbles and District Real Ale Society). They decided to hold a Beer Festival in the village and joined forces with Swansea CAMRA. The Ostreme Hall was booked and in August 1997 the first festival was underway. The event has gone from strength to strength and has become an important part of the Mumbles social calendar. As well as providing a bewildering variety of different ales, the festival features live music and even magic shows. The festival has also recognised important local anniversaries – as well as the centenary of Mumbles Pier in 1998, the fiftieth anniversary of Dylan Thomas's death was celebrated in 2003 and the bicentennial of the Mumbles Railway in 2004. Local celebrities have opened the festival each year by pulling a pint of specially brewed ale. In 1999 there was great hilarity when Cyril the Swan (mascot of Swansea City FC) performed the honours. In the same year, the festival made national headlines when a local bridal party called in to the festival on the way to the church! The festival supports the Mumbles Lifeboat and celebrates its tenth event in 2006.

Right: The Victoria Inn, around the 1930s. The pub's first licence was granted to Robert Howells in 1868 and in 1872 he was charged with permitting gambling. Sergeant Baker said he went to the skittle-alley on the premises, finding two men playing. One said 'That's a quart I've lost now!' They then played for another quart. The defendant said he wasn't aware that the men were playing skittles for beer. The magistrates gave him the benefit of the doubt and discharged him. There was another betting raid many years later in 1938, but that's another story! The Vic was a Hancock's pub from the 1920s and Glyn Maggs was licensee from the 1930s to the 1950s, while also working for Hancocks in Swansea.

Below: The Victoria Inn Bowls Club, 1946. From left to right, back row: T. Williams, C. Mayfield, L. Chambert, W. Hyland, G.H. Elliott (Chairman), A.H. Sparrow, W.J. Ackland (Treasurer), H. Bevan, B.C. Cumings, H. Ashworth (Vice Chairman), H. Jones, T. Price, W. Sheldon. Front row: A. Wood, G. Williams, A.H. Pryer, W.K. David (Secretary), F.T. Churchill (President), S. Fulford (Captain), H. Tegman, R.S. Edwards, T.E. Cuming.

Left: Leading Seaman Alec Hunt RN, who lost his life at the Battle of Narvik in 1940. He'd visited the Victoria Inn while home on leave and written his name on the wall in the bar. Shortly afterwards, Corporal Legg of the Royal Sussex Regiment also wrote his name on the wall and was later killed in action in the desert. 'Captain Jack' Williams of Park Street, a master in the Merchant Navy, had survived several Atlantic convoys. On his last night of leave he added his name to the list shouting 'here's one who's coming back!' His wife, Freda, was horrified when told and returned after closing time to rub his name off. A week later, Captain Jack's ship was torpedoed and the ship was sunk with the loss of many of the crew, but Jack was picked up. He always claimed Freda had saved his life.

Below: The successful Victoria Inn Ladies' Darts team, 1983. From left to right, back row: Tessa Gammon, Daphne Creswell, Violet Bates, Stevie Poole, Yvonne Woolacott, Pat Evans, Anne Evans. Front row: Gail Kilburn, Gwyneth Gammon, Margaret Thrush, Carol Holahan (landlady and captain who won the Welsh Brewers Singles 1982-83).

The house on the right at No. 2 Upper Church Parks gives no clue to its past as the Oddfellows Inn. The pub traded from the 1860s until 1908 and was a 'cottage inn', serving mariners and oyster fishermen. In 1870, licensee Henry Evans was refused a spirit licence and the Oddfellows remained a beerhouse. The Oystermouth Castle Lodge of Oddfellows was formed in 1859 and an Oddfellows Hall was opened in The Dunns in 1888. The pub landlord from 1874 to 1887, William Powell, was himself an Oddfellow, and a well-known oyster dealer and skiff owner. The pub was 'a very small house and poor building, approached through a long garden', and due to the proximity of other pubs was closed by the Compensation Authority in 1908. Compensation of £450 was paid as follows: Licensee, Edwin Gully, £44; Owner, Swansea United Breweries, £145; Lessee, Charles Lloyd Watkins, £261.

This cottage in Western Lane called *Yr Hen Dy Cwrw* (The Old Beer House) was a pub called the Hill House in the second half of the nineteenth century. There was another pub a little further up the lane in the 1840s which had its own malthouse and this may have been an earlier location for the Hill House. There was also a brewhouse at nearby Plunch Lane. In 1862, landlord John Michael was charged with allowing late drinking at the Hill House. PC6 of the County Constabulary visited the house at 12.15 a.m. and found people drinking and dancing there. The defendant said the clock had stopped and he didn't know the time. The bench called this an absurd story and fined him 20s plus costs. In 1881, 'Tom the Fiddler' lived in the cottage next door, and one can imagine him playing his fiddle in the bar. People visiting Mumbles Hill for the fresh air and views were able to enter the pub by a back gate, but the police eventually objected to the licence, claiming it was a troublesome house. It was referred for compensation and closed in 1907. It became a shop for much of the twentieth century and is now a private house.

Opposite: Somerset House became more respectable in the 1880s, serving teas to large Sunday school parties. It became a gentleman's residence and during the Second World War it served as a billet for Army officers when there were 'ack-ack' guns on the hill. It later became a guest house, then a nursing home. It has recently been splendidly restored and renamed Mumbles Hill House – Somerset House wasn't retained because it has thirteen letters.

This poem was composed by an old wayfarer on the Mumbles Hill, July 1853, on reaching a house conspicuously inscribed, 'John Pugh, Licensed to Sell Beer and Porter', but which proved to be uninhabited:

Some speculative *Pugh*
Came up this hill to brew,
And fill the jackets blue
With excellent *cwrw*,
At a welcome sea 'Halloo!'
Nor did the man beshrew
Jerkins of any hue,
He might with ale imbue –
But it seems it wouldn't do.
Doubtless too well he knew,
When bills were falling due,
A lanky purse he'd rue;
So wisely sought anew
Some less exalted mew,
Where money might accrue –
For when the cold winds blew,
The ale-imbibing crew
This bleak hill did eschew:
Thus customers were few –

And worse and worse it grew,
As fewer jugs he drew;
Till off at last flew,
Most likely in a stew,
And bade the hill adieu.
But I, perhaps askew,
His fancied course pursue,
Which may'nt be over true –
As I've no other clue
Than this blank house of *Pugh*,
With its promise in my view
Of 'Beer and Porter' too –
Though a vacant room or two,
That sunbeams wander through,
And naught, save evening dew,
That barely wets my shoe,
My parch'd lips to unglue,
Is here for me, and you,
O much be-rhymed *John Pugh*!

There's nothing worse than a pub with no beer! This was Somerset House on Mumbles Hill, built in 1849. Apparently, the beerhouse was in business again by the 1860s when the licensee was Tom Lloyd, better known as 'Tom the Fiddler'. He did well in the summer months and many were the dances which he organised on the green in front, no doubt playing his famous fiddle! Tommy couldn't keep within the law and was convicted for selling beer on Sundays. He had to give up the house after keeping it for five years. He was a notorious Mumbles character and made the acquaintance of the police courts for drunkenness no less than fifty times!

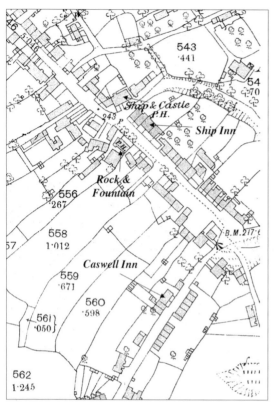

Left: This 1877 map shows the location of Newton's four pubs. The old Ship Inn was probably the earliest pub in the village and in 1827, John Davies, Master Mariner, was its innkeeper. He moved to the Ship and Castle (now the Newton Inn) and the Ship Inn closed in 1860. The small pub in Nottage Road was called the Caswell Inn, located at No. 30 Nottage Road, opposite Woollacott's shop. In 1869, the Caswell Inn's beerhouse licence renewal was refused because of improper notice given and that seems to have been the end of it. The property was renovated in the late 1980s and the old rear portion, where the inn had been, was demolished.

Below: The old Newton Garage was once the location of the Ship Inn. The old garage and cottages alongside were demolished in 1972 to make way for the present Newton Garage.

The Ship and Castle Hotel, Newton, with the Heckler family and maid outside, *c*. 1920. The pub was established in the early 1840s by Captain John Davies who previously kept the nearby Ship Inn. He was still running the Ship and Castle in 1861 at seventy-eight years of age. In 1900 a ploughing competition was held at Richard Woollacott's farm in Thistleboon and in the evening the farmers congregated at the Ship and Castle for supper, speeches and music – 'a good time was had by all'. By 1904, however, the house had 'very primitive sanitary arrangements and very little trade' and the licence was opposed, but Alfred Vivian took over in 1906 and improved things considerably. Ownership was transferred from Swansea Old Brewery to Hancocks in 1912, and the beer was delivered by horse-drawn dray up the steep hill, with flagon deliveries carried out from the converted stables. In 1927 the Justices approved a change of name to the Newton Inn because of the conviction of the Ship and Castle in Mumbles 'for permitting their premises to be used as a brothel'. They were obviously keen to deter undesirable customers! In 1936, Iorwerth Evans became licensee. Including his war service, when wife Millie took over, Iory, as he was known, was tenant for nearly forty years. Iory used to say 'nobody can come into the Newton Inn and be lonely'.

Daniel Jones, the famous musician and composer and lifelong friend of Dylan Thomas, relaxes at the Newton Inn in 1966. 'Doctor Dan' lived in Newton village until his death in 1993 and the Newton Inn was his favourite local.

Ted & Muriel wish customers old and new
Xmas and New Year Greetings

NEWTON INN
NEWTON
TEL: 68329

Good selection of Worthington Beers.
Draught Bass — Carling Lager always available

An advertisement from Christmas 1982, when Ted and Muriel Hancock were licensees. During Ted's time there were many trips arranged by the regulars including steamer trips to 'Combe. The legendary Martin Twomey, of Caswell Riding Stables, was a regular on these trips and 'Captain Jack' would often join them at the pier.

Above and below: Newton Village in 1915 (above) with the Rock and Fountain behind the tree on the left. There was a fire at the Rock sometime after this picture was taken and the fire cart from Mumbles couldn't make it up the hill! The village pump had to be used by a line of all the available men with buckets (and boys returning empty buckets) to extinguish the blaze. The top storey was rebuilt after this with gables shown in the later picture (below) in which the village pump can be seen in front of the post office.

"Rock & Fountain" Newton
Established in 1750 as Brewer, Farmer
Undertaker and Wheelwright.

Above: The Rock and Fountain, sketched after Courage acquired it in 1970, and captioned 'Established in 1750 as Brewer, Farmer, Undertaker and Wheelwright'. John Woollacott became the 'Victuler' in 1836 and ran the farm behind the pub. He was born in Devon in 1810 and was a member of the Woollacott family that settled and farmed in the area. His son, Richard, followed him as licensee and he, in turn, left the inn to his son, Thomas Woollacott. Thomas's wife, Louisa, kept it following his death and then sold the pub after the Second World War. The Rock was in the Woollacott family for 111 years. A family member remembers colliers from the Rhondda camping at Caswell Bay for their holidays. They used to drink day and night in the Rock, where the beer was home-brewed, and on their way out would sometimes fall into the stream outside! Beer was brewed on the premises up to the start of the Second World War. The Woollacott family took over again in 2004, restoring the family name above the door. One of the Rock's regulars is Margaret Thrush, a colourful village character who has collected many thousands of pounds for charity. Margaret celebrates fifty years of charity work in 2006.

Opposite above: In 1856, Henry Crawshay of the wealthy Merthyr ironmasters family, built a marine villa at Langland Bay which was named Llan-y-llan. The house was later to become the Langland Bay Hotel. This 1864 photograph shows the original two-storey house with its tower extending to a third storey.

Opposite below: Langland Bay in 1880, showing the imposing house with its tower, and the coach house and stables to the left, fronted by a walled garden. In 1887, a syndicate called the Langland Bay Co. bought the property to convert it into a grand hotel. The hotel opened in 1889 with fifty rooms, set in fifty acres of land, with a splendid outlook overlooking the bay.

Langland Bay Hotel

Near **Swansea.**

The Mentone of Wales.

Miss LOGAN, Manageress.

In 1922, the hotel was acquired by the Working Men's Club and Institute Union and the main building was converted into a convalescent home. The grand opening ceremony attracted 1,500 club members, with speeches and a brass band playing. It was ironic that the iron magnate's seaside residence became a home for unfortunate men of the class he employed. The annexe and coach house became the new non-residential Langland Bay Hotel and this picture shows the public house and restaurant with the towers of the convalescent home behind. The hotel in its new guise enjoyed great popularity with dinner parties, tea dances and functions of all kinds. It had a magnificent ballroom and could cater for 500 people. Mrs Murison managed the hotel between the 1920s and '50s and recalled many famous visitors from the earlier days, including George Robey and Ramsay MacDonald, when he was Prime Minister. Sadly the days of social activity were not to last – the latter hotel buildings were pulled down in 1989, and seafront apartments were built, aptly named Crawshay Court. The convalescent home closed in 2004, but the main building still stands, proudly dominating the bay.

Opposite above: The hotel initially did very good business and was enlarged to three storeys to increase its capacity. Tennis courts were laid out, and this advertisement of 1903 shows the magnificent structure after its completion. Adjacent land became the Langland Bay golf course in 1904, with the clubhouse conveniently situated at the hotel.

Opposite below: This picture of 1905 shows the hotel from an unusual angle, revealing activity in the stable yard. The hotel was put up for auction around this time amid clear signs that its profitability didn't match up to its palatial appearance. The only bid was for £5,000, a fraction of the vast amount that had been invested. The lot was withdrawn, but within a month, the hotel was sold to Mr Morgan Walters of Llandrindod Wells.

Osborne Cottage was built around 1850 and was the seaside residence of the Richardson family. A Temperance Hotel was established there in 1887 and there were full visitor lists with many people flocking to Mumbles and Langland. In 1891, Annie Jenkins was granted an alehouse licence for the Osborne Hotel and expansion proceeded. During excavations for the hotel extensions, a bone-cave was discovered containing the remains of mammoth, hyena, lion, cave bear and other prehistoric creatures.

This picture shows the extended Osborne Hotel building adjoining the cottage in 1899. In 1897, Alfred Sisley, the French Impressionist painter, stayed at the Osborne, and painted some superb coastal scenes. In 1903, the new St Peter's church at nearby Newton was consecrated and a public luncheon was held at the Osborne to celebrate the event.

The cottage was enlarged by 1909 and the hotel and cottage were sold in 1912 for £4,000, when the hotel had fifteen bedrooms and the cottage was described as 'a bijou seaside residence'. This picture shows the Osborne Hotel and Fairhaven Private Hotel (formerly the Rotherslade Hotel) from the beach.

The Osborne Hotel in the early 1990s, by which time it had been much extended. Many famous sporting teams visited during its heyday, including the 1952 Grand Slam winning Welsh rugby team, the 1963 All Blacks team and George Best and the Northern Ireland football team in 1970. Other famous guests included Harry Secombe, Jimmy Edwards, Ken Dodd, Frankie Howerd and Pam Ayres. Sadly, the hotel's magnificent position made it ripe for redevelopment and it closed in 2000. After being closed for three years, it was demolished and luxury apartments now occupy the site.

Rotherslade
Hotel
LANGLAND BAY,
Near SWANSEA.

HULLY LICENSED. Charmingly situated in its own grounds, overlooking the Sea, commanding a fine view of the Bay and Channel. Convenient for Bathing, Boating and Fishing. Entirely sheltered from easterly winds. Highly recommended by the Medical Profession. Excellent Cuisine.

Telegrams :—Rotherslade Hotel, Langland Bay, Swansea.

For Terms, etc., apply to
THE PROPRIETRESS.

This advertisement for the Rotherslade Hotel was published in a 1903 guide. The hotel was established by 1894 but was a Temperance Hotel until the proprietress, Madam Ana Mitchell, was granted a licence in 1899. The best days of the hotel were during the Edwardian period when performers from Mumbles Pier were brought in to entertain guests in the hotel grounds. The hotel was owned by the Jenkins family and managed in conjunction with the Osborne Hotel. Although summer business was very good, the hotel closed in the wintertime. The licence was not renewed after 1912 and it became the Fairhaven Private Hotel. The building was eventually demolished to make way for luxury flats, and the residents of Fairhaven Court now enjoy the sea views once admired by the hotel guests.

Langland Court Hotel

ON THE GOWER COAST, OVERLOOKING THE BEAUTIFUL BAY OF LANGLAND

delightful

Appointed R.A.C., R.S.A.C. and A.A.

Golf and Tennis nearby
Billiards TSDY "Court
Jester" for Game Fishing
and Cruising Banqueting
and Conference Rooms
Up to 130 catered for
Ample Car Park and
Lock up Garages
T.V. Lounge
Members of the Welsh
Tourist Board
British Hotels,
Restaurants and Caterers
Association.

Langland Court Road,
Langland Bay, Swansea,
Tel: Swansea (0792) 66425 - 68505

Fully Licensed. Brochures available. All Amenities.
Resident Proprietors:
Mr. and Mrs. Arthur E. Birt, M.H.C.I.

The Langland Court Hotel was built at the turn of the nineteenth century and was originally a private house called Lomey. It became a Country Club in the late 1940s, and in 1955 was acquired by the Birt family, who converted it into a popular residential and function hotel. It was granted an on-licence in 1971. Sadly it closed in 2002, with plans to convert the building into apartments, but it was destroyed by fire in late 2005.

This early engraving of Caswell Bay shows the villa that became the Caswell Bay Hotel. The house was built around 1850, and in 1860 the hotel was described as 'a large and handsome structure, well furnished and appointed, with every accommodation and conducted by Miss Jordan, the house having been originally built, at considerable cost, by her brother'. The hotel became fully licensed in 1863.

If you appreciate Lovely Walks, Beautiful Bays, Safe Bathing and Golf

Stay at the

CASWELL BAY HOTEL - Caswell

Unique Situation   (Fully Licensed)   Overlooking and facing Sea

Overlooking prettiest Bay on the Coast. 3 Golf Courses within easy distance

Most beautifully situated Hotel in Gower

Illustrated Tariff on application. *Telephone:* Mumbles 6184. *Telegrams:* "Hinds Caswell Mumbles"

This advertisement from 1936 shows the hotel's beautiful location overlooking the bay. In 1917, the hotel suffered a theft from its wine cellar – three Mumbles men gained access from the coal cellar (two of them worked for the coal merchant!). All three were fined. After the Second World War, the hotel underwent numerous structural alterations and by 1958 was 'the largest hotel on the Gower Coast'.

A closer view of the Caswell Bay Hotel in the 1950s, which in its heyday hosted many functions including wedding receptions, parties and dinner dances. In 1953, the touring New Zealand rugby team were entertained there by Swansea businessmen. The ballroom seating capacity was 200, with numerous other function rooms. In 1980 the Beach Bar became Onedins, a popular young people's venue. Sadly, in 1990, the hotel was demolished to make way for luxury flats, ending its 140-year life.

four

South
Gower

The Plough and Harrow, Murton, with thatched roof, in 1890. The pub is reputed to be one of the oldest in Gower, dating from the sixteenth century. In 1827 the innkeeper was John Hoskin, and by 1844 John Davies held the licence. When the Bishopston Mapsant (Saint's Day) was celebrated on 22 February 1864, festivities took place at the Plough, and 'Tom the Fiddler' from Mumbles performed. John Davies met a tragic end in 1870 when he was thrown from his horse and died from his injuries. His funeral at Oystermouth was one of the largest known in the district. The other pub in the village was the Mansel Arms near the village green, carried on by Lemuel Thomas. This closed in 1874 after a fairly brief existence. As its name suggests, the Plough was very much associated with the local farming community. In the first half of the twentieth century it hosted numerous gatherings following ploughing matches in the area.

Opposite above: The Plough and Harrow in 1920, with the old thatched roof gone following rebuilding, and beer supplied by Swansea Old Brewery. David John Thomas bought the pub from the brewery in 1910 and his family ran the pub until 1978, overseeing numerous alterations and improvements.

Opposite below: Mr and Mrs Alan Davies of the Plough and Harrow, Murton, on their retirement in 1978. The old-established free house then transferred from private ownership to Wessex Taverns (Grand Met), and shortly afterwards the pub was extended and renovated.

The Bishopston Valley Hotel in the early 1900s. This alehouse was originally called the Cross Inn as it was situated at the old village crossroads. In 1827, the innkeeper was David Phillip and in 1864 it was bought by John Bevan. Apparently, he named it the California Inn after he returned from living in California. By 1877 it was known as the Valley Hotel and was later rebuilt in the distinctive style we see today.

A meeting of the Court Leet at the Valley Hotel, *c.* 1920. From left to right: Will Griffiths-Mansel, Will Jones (Rock House), Harry Lloyd (The Forge), -?-, ? Davies (Rate Collector), Farmer Webborn, -?- (Farmer Webborn's son; Ale Taster?). Courts Leet were ancient manorial courts which dealt with local issues and minor criminal matters. The ale-tasters were early weights and measures officers who monitored the brewing, quality and price of ale. By the 1920s their function was largely ceremonial. One of the last Courts Leet held at the Valley Hotel was recalled by George Long: 'when all presentments had been dealt with, the company retired to the converted barn across the yard, there to be regaled with a monumental meal, the deputy steward and the agent carving at two huge joints of meat, one at each end of the table'.

Opposite below: The Bishopston Valley Hotel, showing the old barn alongside which later became the Forge Restaurant. By 1937, Hancock's Brewery had an interest, and between 1964 and 1976 the popular Jack Bartlett was landlord. He was previously manager of the Pier Hotel in Mumbles and became a Swansea City councillor. After his days, it was said at the Valley that 'when the door creaks, that's Jack coming in!'

Carnival day outside the Joiners Arms, Bishopston, in the 1920s. The processions started from the Joiners, parading through the village to Murton Green, where the carnival events were held. The Joiners Arms was probably established by William Lloyd, who was the village carpenter, wheelwright and blacksmith. He was granted a full alehouse licence in 1862, although the premises may have been a beerhouse for a few years before that. There is evidence of a smithy on the site in 1802. The Shoe Inn down the lane closed in 1858, so the Joiners probably took some of its trade. William Lloyd was still the landlord at the Joiners in 1901, and was also a carriage builder and parish clerk. The front part of the Joiners is probably the original pub, with the rear extension built over the old carpenter's and blacksmith's yard.

Above: William Lewis and a large group of well-dressed regulars outside the Joiners Arms, Bishopston, in the 1920s. In more modern times, the Joiners has enjoyed success as a real ale outlet, winning the CAMRA Pub of the Year award three times, including the South and Mid-Wales regional award in 1999.

Right: The Swansea Brewing Co. was established by Rory Gowland at the Joiners Arms in 1996, restoring brewing to Gower some sixty years after brewing ceased in Reynoldston. Ales with local names such as Three Cliffs Gold, Pwlldu XXXX and St Teilo's Tipple proved very popular. Interestingly, St Teilo's church tower clock came from the Old Brewery in Singleton Street, Swansea, and was installed in 1886. The Swansea Brewing Co. celebrates its tenth anniversary in 2006.

The Malthouse at Bishopston was in operation in the nineteenth century. The malt produced from barley was supplied to numerous public houses in Gower and to farmers brewing their own beer. The maltster in the 1840s and '50s was Thomas Edwards, who also kept the Shoe Inn for a period. The Shoe Inn was just across the main road, alongside the parish pound, and in 1827 David Daniel was its innkeeper. In 1841 an auction for the nearby Pennard Mill was held there. The Shoe Inn closed in 1858 but the malthouse was still going in the late 1870s.

Opposite above: The Beaufort Arms in Kittle, sometime in the early 1900s. There were two Beaufort alehouses in Pennard parish in 1827 (the other was at Pwlldu). The Beaufort is reputed to be ancient – the pub sign records a date of 1460! Perhaps it was a hostelry for early travellers. In the middle of the 1800s, the Collins family kept it for over three decades and it was referred to as 'Collinses'. An inquest was held there for a Pennard farmer's wife in 1917 – sadly, the verdict was 'died from self-administered poison'. More recently (and more happily) during Harold Thomas's time as landlord, someone won a duck as third prize in the Christmas raffle. Harold produced a live duck which ended up flying around the bar!

Kittle Green, with the Beaufort Arms on the left, in 1915. One of the other two houses was probably the earlier Kittle Inn, recorded in 1827. The annual Kittle Fair was one of the highlights of the village in the nineteenth century, with crowds of Gower farmers and stock dealers bartering on the green, and many side shows. The special 'fair cakes', baked in the old brick oven at the Beaufort, were very popular with fairgoers. These were large spiced buns threaded on long canes, and no one visiting the fair would leave without sampling them.

Pwlldu and Valley

Above: Pwlldu was once a thriving little port where limestone quarried from the cliffs was transported across to Devon. The picture shows Pwlldu, with the old Ship Inn on the left and the Beaufort Arms to the right. The little malthouse in the centre served both pubs and is said to have changed hands between them over a game of cards! The pubs supported the limestone trade, with quarrymen favouring the Ship and mariners the Beaufort. The Jenkins family were running the Ship (then known as 'Pooldie House') from the 1700s, and licensee John Jenkins was also a quarryman. He is said to have witnessed the wrecking of the *Caesar* in 1760 when sixty-eight people, including press-ganged men, were drowned at Pwlldu Head. The dead were buried in a mass grave nearby known as Gravesend. A happier outcome befell the crew of the barque *Lammershagen* when she ended her days on the rocks in 1882 – the captain and eighteen-man crew all came ashore safely and were put up in the Beaufort. The area had strong smuggling connections and nearby Brandy Cove is aptly named. No doubt some of the contraband found its way into the bars of the two inns as well as other pubs in the Bishopston valley, such as the New Inn, the Bull and the Star, which are lost in the mists of time.

Opposite above: The Beaufort dates from before 1827, and the Jones family were licensees for much of the nineteenth century. Shooting parties from the big houses visited Bishopston Valley and took refreshment at the Beaufort. The picture shows two 'toffs' with an old local at the turn of the century. Jane Jones, licensee at that time, was a much-loved character known locally as Aunt Jane. She died tragically in 1907, falling down an open manhole when visiting a Swansea brewery. The Beaufort Arms closed in 1939 and is now privately owned.

Opposite below: The Ship's alehouse licence expired in 1863; David Jenkins was the last licensee. This picture dates from the 1890s when the quarries behind were winding down and the Ship became Tea Rooms. The Jenkins family remained until the late 1970s, having lived there for 250 years. Ship Cottage is now a private house.

GOWER INN PARKMILL GOWER

In 1824, the *Cambrian* advertised 'a new, spacious, well finished public house, with stables, coach house, piggery and large garden known as the Gower Inn, in the centre of Gower'. It was built by Thomas Penrice, and this picture dates from 1907. The inn at Parkmill became one of the best known hostelries in Gower. It was a central meeting place for many, including farmers on their way to Swansea market and drovers collecting their cattle, paying for them in gold sovereigns. It was also a place of refreshment for the early horse-buses at the halfway point of their journey. In 1889 however, John Grove was charged with furious driving and drunkenness. He was driving his horse bus at a mad rate down the hill from Kilvrough until his career was stopped by a wall near the Gower Inn, where he, his horses, and his brake, came to grief. Several persons near the inn had a narrow escape from being run over and the Mumbles Brass Band, returning from a picnic at Reynoldston, narrowly escaped annihilation! Grove said, 'I was not drunk, only a little excited'. He was fined £10.

GOWER · INN · PARKMILL

he above HOSTLERY is situated in the most Picturesque Parts of GOWER (five miles distant from the MUMBLES and eight from SWANSEA), where 'arties can be provided with the best of Accommodation, Upon the most reasonable terms.

TRAVELERS SPECIALLY ATTENDED TO.

BEDS.

Proprietor, JOHN JAMES SCOTT.

The Gower Inn was popular with tourists due to its picturesque location, as this advertisement of 1884 shows. In the 1860s, proprietor Edward Webb was known for his magnificent display of flowers, and was said to be prouder of his garden than his hotel. His roses and hollyhocks were 'unequalled'.

The charabancs were soon calling at the Gower Inn. There were many functions held, including feasts, dances and smoking concerts. At one concert in 1922, the invited Swansea artiste couldn't make it and a local boy who 'spoke like a poet' was pressed into service at the last moment. The well-known Gower poet, Cyril Gwynn, gave his first public performance. Another well-known poet, Dylan Thomas, visited in 1932.

The ivy-clad Gower Inn in 1947. The inn has seen many changes during its 180 years – the old stables are now a restaurant and the once-celebrated rose garden is the car park.

Landlady Hannah Thomas in the doorway of the New Inn, Parkmill, *c.* 1905. The New Inn was recorded in 1811, and was near to Stonemill, the other ancient mill in the village. In 1904, Hannah's son, David, tragically died after losing his footing in a trap when his pony moved, and falling to the road, striking his head. The New Inn closed a few years later, and is now known as New Inn Cottage. Other lost inns in the parish include the Sovereign at Lunnon and the Farmers Arms in Ilston.

This cottage and shop at Oxwich, pictured around the 1950s, was once the Bull Inn, a focal point for the small community engaged in farming, fishing, quarrying (and a little smuggling!). In 1824, Matilda Bevan was innkeeper, and later Thomas Gibbs. He was a champion prize-fighter at Penrice Fairs, where the rival tavern was the King's Head. Quarrying ended in 1899, marking the closure of the Bull – it is said the licence was allowed to expire by the Penrice Estate.

In 1789, Mr Talbot built a new rectory at Oxwich for Revd John Collins. The earlier rectory was destroyed in a storm. The rectory became Cliffside Guest House, pictured here sometime in the 1950s, and later became the Oxwich Bay Hotel. John Collins was prophetic when he wrote in 1807 that, 'ere long an Inn, Hotel or Tavern will afford accommodation for travellers'. Little did he know that two centuries later, his rectory would be the hotel.

Above: The King Arthur Hotel and Reynoldston Fair, around the 1880s. Harvest Fairs started on the Higher Green in about 1860, after Mr Talbot stopped the Fair at Penrice due to the brutality of the prize-fighting. The King Arthur was built in 1870, at half its present size, near the earlier Rising Sun Inn which dated back to the 1700s. William Tucker was the first licensee of the hotel. He'd previously been charged with assault at the Rising Sun – he said that, it being Fair Day, he'd taken two or three glasses of whisky!

Left: This advertisement dates from 1886. John Bevan enlarged the hotel in 1889 and started running a brake service to Killay and Swansea. A serious accident happened when he was returning home in the trap and the horse bolted, throwing him out into the road. He sustained severe injuries but recovered and was still running the hotel at the turn of the twentieth century.

A horse bus outside the King Arthur, *c*. 1906. The hotel is named after Arthur's Stone, a prominent megalithic tomb on nearby Cefn Bryn, reputed to be a pebble from King Arthur's shoe which he cast away onto the Bryn. The hotel became very popular with excursionists, and in 1911 the staff of Rees and Kirby visited the hotel for dinner and tea and held a tug-of-war and cricket match. In 1920, Violet Howell took over, a commanding personality known as the 'Queen of Gower'. The hotel was a regular rendezvous for motorists in the 1930s and after the war many organisations held functions there during the heyday of dinner dances.

Mrs Joan Sparkes, Vice-Chairman of the West Wales Muscular Dystrophy branch, receives a cheque and invalid chair from 'Mine Host' Leslie Fisher, and members of the King Arthur Hotel Gardening Club in 1972. The regulars raised £114 from an auction of produce.

Reynoldston Brewery on the Lower Green, sometime in the 1890s. The brewery was operating by the 1870s and continued until the 1930s. In its later days it was a beer shop and butchery business, and beer was delivered with the meat! In 1889, the brewer, Glyn James, announced he would treat local residents to a feast of free beer and bread and cheese on Cefn Bryn. When the day arrived, the astonished residents saw a large barrel of beer and countless loaves, with a 'regiment of cheeses' leaving the brewery in a cart for the top of Cefn Bryn, where the event was accompanied by horse races and much conviviality. Mr James was toasted as a man of enterprise, deserving of success for his hospitality, although some residents thought the bacchanalian feast degrading! The brewery was run by Swansea Old Brewery in 1900, when an eighteen-gallon cask purchased by Penmaen Workhouse cost 20s. Hancock's took over in 1928 but terminated their lease in 1933. In the 1970s the old brewery was a craft shop, and is now a private cottage. As well as the brewery, there was an earlier malthouse at the western side of Lower Green, where Box Farm is situated. This was established in 1829, and became an alehouse called the Maltsters' Arms. Thomas Davies was the maltster between 1838 and 1875.

The Ship Inn, Porteynon, at the turn of the century, when Harriet Hughes was landlady. Porteynon was once a thriving port, with limestone quarrying, oyster fishing and the smuggling fraternity trying to keep a step ahead of the excise men. Curtis Grove's rhyme sums it up nicely:

Yesteryear Port Eynon Bay
Saw much of lime and pillage,
Livelihood was of the sea
With five pubs in the village

Other pubs in the village were the Britannia, the Hope and Anchor and the Sea Fencible, with Samuel Gibbs's Malthouse on the front. The Sea Fencibles were the Home Guard of Napoleonic times, when there was widespread fear of a French invasion. Isaac Stote was the Ship's landlord in the old smuggling days, followed in the 1850s by John Bevan. John accommodated some survivors from the brigantine *Perie* when she was wrecked on Skysea in 1864, but his house was described at the time as 'a diabolical one'! The summer visitors started arriving in the 1880s, and in 1909 John Grove started Gower's first motor-bus service from the Ship Inn to Swansea. The Ship is the only village pub remaining but the summer visitors keep returning.

Left: This group outside the Ship, seen here around 1938, includes, from left to right: Mr White, Harry Phillips, George Eynon, -?-, William Roberts Snr, -?-, Haydn Jones, -?-. The gentleman in the foreground and the others wearing shorts are probably tourists.

Below: The former Black Lion in Overton, probably painted by Edward Duncan Jnr, *c.* 1890. The building was demolished in 1898 and Lilac House now stands on the site. David Beynon was a maltster at Overton between the 1850s and 1870s, and probably ran the Black Lion. When it closed, Overton villagers had to walk down to Porteynon for their ale (and back up the hill afterwards!).

five

West
Gower

The old Ship Inn at Middleton was kept by the Beynon family for most of the nineteenth century. The inn closed in 1906 when villagers petitioned the Penrice Estate against further letting as a public house. It became Ship Farm and plaques on the farm's front wall indicate the pub was built in 1749 and rebuilt in 1893. It was one of at least three old inns in the village. The Penrice Arms was open until 1847, kept by Samuel Ace who previously kept the Welcome to Town, also in Rhossily parish. There was also the Bulls Eye beerhouse in Sheep Lane. The local smugglers probably had plenty of outlets for their illicit liquor!

Right: Petty Officer Edgar Evans, who tragically perished with Captain Scott on the ill-fated *Terra Nova* expedition to the South Pole in 1912. Evans was closely associated with the Ship Inn, having married the landlord's daughter, his cousin Lois Beynon. Evans was tremendously strong and he once expelled some Swansea troublemakers from the Ship, taking them outside two at a time in such a way that they swore they'd never visit the inn again! His wife, Lois, erected a memorial in his name at Rhossili church bearing the inscription: 'To seek, to strive, to find and not to yield'.

Below: Captain Scott, Edward Wilson and Edgar Evans at Amundsen's tent on 18 January 1912. This photograph captures the despair the party must have felt on finding that Amundsen had reached the South Pole before them. (Courtesy of Canterbury Museum, ref. 19XX.2.639)

Worms Head Cottage.
Rhossilly.

Most lovely situation in
the Gower Peninsula

RHOSSILLY

The WORMSHEAD COTTAGE

PRIVATE HOTEL

BATHING
FISHING
RAMBLING

Overlooking the famous Worms Head and the beautiful Rhossilly Bay. Every convenience. Two Dining Rooms (separate tables). Large Lounge. Twenty Bedrooms

RESIDENT PROPRIETOR - - G. THOMAS

An early picture of the King's Head, Llangennith. The village was described by Dylan Thomas as 'very near to nowhere' but once had four public houses and was pretty lively, particularly when the Mapsant was celebrated on 5 July. The village green was lined with booths and fiddles played outside the taverns while prize-fights, cockfighting, quoits playing and all manner of gambling took place. Large quantities of ale and 'whitepot' (a traditional dish) were consumed. The legendary Celtic Saint, Cenydd, founded a priory here in the sixth century and no doubt hostelries welcomed visitors for centuries. Other village pubs were the Welcome to Town and Town House, while Bank Farm is said to have been the Horse and Jockey. In 1840, the steamer *City of Bristol* was wrecked near Llangennith and sadly twenty-four people drowned. The only two survivors were looked after by William Tucker at the King's Head, where an inquest was also held.

Opposite above: Wormshead Cottage was built around 1880 and early tourists, keen to view the spectacular Worms Head and Rhossili Bay, stayed there, even though the beds were 'hard as granite'! With the advent of motor transport, visitors increased and the cottage became a private hotel and then a Country Club. Dylan Thomas visited in 1953, and called Worms Head 'the great rock … at the end of the humped and serpentine body'. The Worms Head Hotel finally became fully licensed in 1969 after a long battle, the parish having been without a pub since the Ship at Middleton closed sixty-three years earlier. Another pub called the Barley Mow existed in the eighteenth century, when Rhossili was known for smuggling and wrecking.

Opposite below: An advertisement for the rebuilt Wormshead Cottage Hotel, 1936.

The King's Head, *c.* 1921, when George Rees was proprietor. The four little girls are Nancy and Connie Kneath, and Maggie and Evelyn Rees (George's daughters). Also pictured are Edwin Ace, village postmaster, and Vicar Scudamore, from the old parsonage on the beach. The lady in the doorway is probably Mrs Rees. The Rees family owned the King's Head for over a century.

Llangennith village, with the old petrol pump alongside the King's Head, around the 1950s. Buildings on each side of the pub were incorporated as it expanded to cater for the holiday trade from nearby caravan parks and surfing beaches. The pub is reputed to be haunted by an old man and a young girl, but they are benign presences!

Gower folksinger, Phil Tanner (right), at the King's Head in the 1940s. Phil Tanner was born in 1862 into a family of weavers who loved singing and dancing. When he was twenty-five he married the widowed landlady of the Welcome to Town (who was twice his age) and moved into the inn where he no doubt learned many of his songs. His repertoire was vast, with many of the songs collected from travelling tailors and gypsies and other performers like 'Tom the Fiddler' from Mumbles. Phil also acted as 'bidder' at local 'bidding weddings', which have been a Gower custom for centuries. The 'bidder' invites the wedding guests by singing a formal invitation at the homes of those invited. Phil was also able to produce a lively Gower Reel with his 'mouth music'. In his later days, he could often be heard singing at the Kings Head and many of his songs have been recorded for posterity. The 'Gower Nightingale' died at Penmaen in 1950 aged eighty-eight.

Above: Llangennith Green, with the thatched Welcome to Town Inn on the left. In the 1820s, the innkeepers were John and Elizabeth Beynon, and in 1854 William Nicholas took over. His widow, Ruth, later married Phil Tanner, and the sign above the door read:

> Welcome to Town, Ladies and Gentlemen, by Ruth Tanner,
> Licensed to sell Beer, Wine and Spirits,
> Call softly, Drink soberly, Pay freely, Depart quietly,
> I've trusted many to my sorrow, Pay today and trust tomorrow.

Ruth and Phil moved to Lower Mill in 1897, and the Welcome gradually declined. When the licence was refused in 1911, it was in a deplorable state with very little trade. It was later rebuilt and became the Welcome Guest House for a while.

Left: Phil Tanner in front of the old Welcome to Town Inn, still thatched but no longer a pub, around the 1940s.

FROG LANE, GOWER.

This view of Frog Lane, Llanmadoc, shows the old forge in the foreground with the Britannia Inn behind. Next along the lane on the right is the old Mariners Inn, with the Ship Inn opposite. The Farmers Arms was further up the lane. Llanmadoc was a busy little port in the early 1800s when Cheriton Pill was navigable. Maritime business included export of limestone and barley and import of coal (and a fair amount of smuggled goods!). The four taverns catered for the mariners as well as thirsty quarrymen, farmers and weavers. There were no less than six alehouses in Llanmadoc parish in the 1750s, with a further three in neighbouring Cheriton parish, which includes the hamlet of Landimore. Landimore was also a small port sharing in the limestone trade, where the 'Landremore Inn' survived until 1855 and the Three Brothers was still flourishing in the 1880s. The Brandy House, under the tor, was probably the third alehouse, with its obvious smuggling connections.

Frog Lane, with the old Ship Inn on the left and the Mariners' Inn opposite on the right, with a little dray outside the brewhouse. The Ship probably closed by 1850 and Forge Cottage now occupies the site.

The old Mariners Inn and brewhouse, 1908. William Howell was the mariner and innkeeper in the mid-nineteenth century, and the Dolling family continued brewing until the early 1900s. The house is now Fir Tree Cottage.

GLAMORGANSHIRE,
TO WIT.

A T a General Meeting of his Majesty's Justices of the Peace, acting in and for the Hundred of Swansea, in the County of Glamorgan, held at the Guildhall, in the Town of Swansea, in the Hundred and County aforesaid, on Friday, the Twenty-eighth day of September, One Thousand Eight Hundred and Twenty-seven, _George Bowen_ at the Sign of the _Ship_ in the _Parish_ of _Lanmaddock_ in the said Hundred and County, Victualler, acknowledges himself to be indebted to our Sovereign Lord the King, in the Sum of _Thirty_ Pounds _Elisha Walker_ in the said Hundred and County _Parish_ of _Cheriton_ and _Richard Richards_ of _the Parish of Lanmaddock_ in the said Hundred and County, _Mariners_ severally acknowledge themselves to be indebted to our Sovereign Lord the King in the Sum of _Ten_ Pounds each, to be levied upon their several Goods and Chattels, Lands and Tenements, by way of Recognizance, to his Majesty's use, his Heirs, and Successors, upon condition that the said _George Bowen_ do and shall keep the true Assize in uttering and selling Bread and other Victuals, Beer, Ale, and other Liquors, in h House, and shall not fraudulently dilute or adulterate the same, and shall not use, in uttering and selling thereof, any Pots or other Measures that are not of full Size; and shall not wilfully or knowingly permit Drunkenness or Tippling, nor get Drunk in h House or other Premises; nor knowingly suffer any Gaming with Cards, Draughts, Dice, Bagatelle, or any other sedentary Game, in h House, or any of the Out-Houses, Appurtenances, or Easements thereto belonging, by Journeymen, Labourers, Servants, or Apprentices; nor knowingly introduce, permit, or suffer any Ball, Bear, or Badger Baiting, Cock-fighting, or other such Sport or Amusement, in any part of h Premises; nor shall knowingly or designedly, and with a view to harbour and entertain such, permit or suffer Men or Women of notoriously bad fame, or dissolute Girls and Boys, to assemble and meet together, in h House, or any of the Premises thereto belonging; nor shall keep open h House, nor permit or suffer any drinking or tipling in any part of h Premises, during the usual Hours of Divine Service on Sundays; nor shall keep open h House or other Premises, during late Hours of the Night, or early in the Morning, for any other purpose than the Reception of Travellers; but do keep good Rule and Order therein, according to the purport of a Licence granted for selling Ale, Beer, or other Liquors, by Retail, in the said House and Premises, for One whole Year, commencing on the Tenth day of October next; then this Recognizance to be void, or else to remain in full force.

Murray and Rees, Printers, Swansea.

The Alehouse Recognizance of 1827 for the Ship at Lanmaddock. The recognizance required surety that the victualler, George Bowen, would keep to the terms of his licence in the sum of £30, with further sureties of £10 each from Elisha Walker of Cheriton (farmer) and Richard Richards of Lanmaddock (mariner). The requirements included serving full measures, not permitting drunkenness and not allowing gambling. The reference to bull, bear and badger-baiting is a gruesome reminder of the past – cockfighting was abolished in 1849. The item concerning 'men and women of notoriously bad fame' is a reflection that some taverns of the time (and later) had reputations for being disorderly houses. I'm sure that wasn't the case in Llanmadoc!

The Britannia Inn, Llanmadoc, with the old Mariners Inn behind, *c.* 1930. The Britannia has long and happy associations with the Llanmadoc Mapsant, but in 1819 a Methodist minister called the Mapsant an 'ungodly gathering… a meeting of the Devil for drinking and dancing'. In 1834, the Primitive Methodists of Blaenavon sent a missionary to Swansea who spent two months preaching in the area. He included a sermon at the Britannia Inn, which was 'thronged to excess'! In contrast, the celebrated rector of Llanmadoc and Cheriton, the Revd J.D. Davies, was an enthusiastic supporter of village festivities, including the Mapsant. He was also an active member of the Ancient Order of Foresters who held their meetings at the Britannia. The Mapsant continued to be celebrated on 12 November down the years and the tradition has been revived in the village in recent times.

Opposite above: The Britannia Inn, clearly having been discovered by motorists, around the 1930s. The pub faces Llanmadoc Hill, which separates Llanmadoc and Llangennith, also known as 'Penny Hill' because the King's Head is on one side and Britannia on the other!

Opposite below: Les Arnold (right), publican at the Britannia, with regular Glyn Thomas in the early 1960s. The Arnolds took over in 1938 when Hancock's Brewery acquired the Britannia and were 'mine hosts' for around thirty-five years.

The Farmers Arms, Llanmadoc, 1930s. The inn was held by John Guy in 1843. In the Whitford disaster of 1868, around a dozen vessels were battered to pieces by mountainous seas in the Burry estuary. Many men perished, with their bodies washed up with the wreckage on local beaches. Inquests were held at the Farmers Arms on five of the poor fellows. The jury were mainly local farmers, with Revd Davies as foreman. In happier times, the reverend enjoyed the 'very superior mutton pies' provided by Mrs Gwyn for the Mapsant.

Arthur Yeandle, serving Charlie Price and son Alec at the Farmers Arms, in the 1950s. Mr and Mrs Yeandle took over in 1940 and continued the tradition of cooking home-made pies. There was a very convivial atmosphere in the single-bar pub, with the kitchen opened up for sing-songs on Saturday nights. Sadly, the Farmers closed in 1971.

six

North Gower

The Greyhound Inn at Oldwalls – George Roberts was licensee between 1921 and 1952. Samuel Phillips was granted a new alehouse licence at the Greyhound in 1858, although there was a house there before this. Many a weary traveller called in at 'The Dog' for a dobbin of ale in front of a roaring fire, and the old horse buses stopped there in the early 1900s, followed by the Vanguard motorbuses in the 1920s. The pub was also used by farmers visiting the village smithy and wheelwright just along the road. One visitor in 1906 didn't appreciate the hospitality after his party called there for tea. He assaulted landlord James Brockie, striking him a violent blow on the nose, and was fined £2. Today's visitors will find a much-changed pub and restaurant but the welcoming fires are still there to greet them.

An advertisement for the Greyhound Inn from an early 1930s Tourist Guide.

Above: The Dolphin Inn, Llanrhidian, 1930s. It was recorded as an alehouse in 1826, when George Evans was the innkeeper, and probably dates from the eighteenth century. An early landlord was Christopher Badcock, who was implicated in the murder of the toll collector on the North Gower road in 1845. The local Oddfellows Lodge was formed in 1867 and held its first meetings at the Dolphin. The pub was included in Swansea Old Brewery's auction of 1881. After the Second World War, Hancock's Brewery owned the inn and proper toilets were provided in 1949, no doubt appreciated by licensee Mrs Long and her customers! The pub closed its doors in 1995 but the bar and fittings still exist.

Right: In 1975 David Davies, a talented local singer, won the Welsh National Talent competition organised by Welsh Brewers. Regulars from the Dolphin Inn travelled to Blackpool to support him in the National Championship. David is pictured here with the Welsh Brewers' representative (left) and licensees Margaret and Layton Thomas.

The Welcome to Town Inn, Llanrhidian, around the 1920s. The inn probably existed in the eighteenth century and Philip Morris was the innkeeper in 1826. The Welcome was a regular meeting place 'where village statesmen talked with looks profound, and news much older than their ale went round'. The Gower Association for the Prosecution of Felons was formed in 1810 and held its meetings there. This was a group of local landowners and gentry formed to protect property and deal with criminals before the regular police service began. Their last case, sheep-stealing, was in 1856. Llanrhidian hosted regular fairs on the village green, where livestock were sold and wandering musicians played while hawkers sold their wares. The three village pubs must have done a roaring trade! Important activities were held at the Welcome, including the inquests of a pitman killed in a colliery accident in 1869 and a Llanrhidian woman drowned in a local brook in 1906. It was even possible to 'sign the pledge' at the Oddfellows Meeting Room at the Welcome – an unusual activity for a public house! When offered for sale in 1920, the property included a two-stall stable, a cow house, cart house and pigsty. The pub eventually expanded to include the next-door cottage, and in 1988 its two small public rooms were merged, the old village inn becoming a restaurant.

Opposite above: The Welcome to Town in 1937, with the 'whipping stone' on the green. It has been suggested that wrongdoers were chained to the stone as punishment for their misdeeds!

Opposite below: The 'breaking of the bottle' at the Welcome to Town in 1981. The collection by customers raised £200 for the Cheshire Homes. The photograph shows Welsh international rugby stars Mark Wyatt (left) and Roger Blyth prior to cracking the bottle. Also in the picture are joint licensees Mrs Betty Walters and Mrs Pat Cottle.

The New Moon Country Club, pictured here in an advertisement from 1938, had previously been a country house, and by the 1950s was renamed the North Gower Country Club. In 1973 an on-licence was granted and the formerly private club became the fully licensed North Gower Hotel. The extended hotel became well known for its many functions over the years, with resident bands, dining and dancing.

The North Gower Hotel
Llanrhidian

The North Gower Hotel. The hotel has been expanded to include sixteen bedrooms – the original house with the gable end is on the right-hand side of this sketch.

Right: William Thomas (1800-87) was a farmer and the first landlord of the 'Crofte Inn', which was granted a new licence in 1858. The farm dated back to the previous century and no doubt William decided to offer the beer he brewed to visiting seamen shipping coal. Crofty village expanded as coal-working developed locally, with colliers building their houses there. In the early 1900s there were objections to the pub's licence – there was a conviction in 1903 for selling drink to a child, and sanitary arrangements were unsatisfactory, with the urinal 'too far from the premises'. In 1914, the pub consisted of a taproom, parlour, kitchen, cellar and clubroom.

Below: The Crofty Inn Free House 'Take Courage', around the 1960s. The pub was selling Hancock's beers in the 1930s and Buckley's Brewery had an interest in the 1980s.

The old Ship and Castle in Penclawdd, around the late 1920s. Truman's took it over in 1926 and demolished and rebuilt it in the 1930s. The pub occupied a prominent position overlooking the seafront on 'Ship Bank' and Evan Evans was licensee back in 1826, when shipbuilding was going on nearby. Penclawdd's copper works had been established in the eighteenth century, with the tinplate works arriving a century later. At its height, Penclawdd boasted many public houses, mainly along the foreshore. From west to east were the Traveller's Rest (closed in 1906), Glanmor Inn (closed in 1914), George Inn (closed in 1906), Ship and Castle, Royal Oak, White House (closed in 1905), Coasting Pilot (closed in 1914) and Railway Inn, with the Colliers Arms at Penylan (closed in 1874). Some of these were just 'parlour pubs', but the Ship and Castle was a large house, with stables and a club room used for picnic parties and Foresters Friendly Society meetings.

Opposite above: Penclawdd has long been famous for rugby. When William Davies was landlord of the Ship and Castle, his son, Willie Davies, formed the famous 'schoolboy half-back' partnership with his cousin, Haydn Tanner. They played together for Swansea when the mighty All Blacks were defeated in 1935, and also for Wales. The Ship was headquarters for Penclawdd Rugby Club for years, with the changing rooms and tubs in the pub, and great sing-songs after the game (and many pints downed!). The picture shows Penclawdd RFC 1933/34 outside the Ship and Castle, with Willie Davies (front row, second from left) and Haydn Tanner (front row, right) next to Bryn Evans, Penclawdd's first international cap.

Opposite below: The Ship and Castle, after rebuilding by Truman's in the 1930s. Sadly, the pub closed around 1990 and was demolished to make way for new houses.

David Jenkins was granted a licence at the Oddfellows Arms in Benson Street, Penclawdd, in 1863, a few years before the arrival of the railway. The Oddfellows was demolished in 1877 to make way for the railway extension from Penclawdd to Llanmorlais, and was rebuilt in its present location, being renamed the Railway Inn in 1882. Described as 'the best house in the place' in 1906, it had a bar, smoke room, tap room and commercial room and good stables and coach house. John and Ann Roberts had taken over in 1904 and kept the Railway until 1939. 'Mrs Roberts y Railway' was an old-style landlady who stood no nonsense and often physically threw out customers for swearing or drinking too much. However, Mrs Roberts looked after the commercial travellers staying at the inn very well and 'kept a good pantry' The picture probably dates from the early 1930s.

Opposite above: The Royal Oak, Penclawdd, *c.* 1940s. This beerhouse near the seafront was in business by the 1860s, by which time the famed cockle industry was well-established. Groups of women with donkeys raked and sieved the shellfish from the mudflats of the estuary and brought them to the foreshore near the Royal Oak for boiling on hand-made grates, before carrying them to market. Hancock's leased the Royal Oak from 1891 and considered the house to be a good centre for the flagon trade. A flagon store, stable and cart shed were established in 1912 at a cost of £180. Edgar Tucker became landlord in 1923 and his son, Wilfred, delivered the flagons around Gower. A full licence was not obtained until 1960, just before Edgar retired.

Opposite below: Edgar Tucker serving Hancock's cask beer at the Royal Oak, Penclawdd.

The Coasting Pilot Inn, on the track to Llotrog, was one of Penclawdd's early beerhouses, recorded in 1826. It was leased to Felinfoel brewery in 1906, when it consisted of two tenements with two passages leading in and no less than five doors! The Justices decided in 1914 that it was no longer required, as the tin works had been dismantled some years earlier. It was closed and became two cottages, later converted to three.

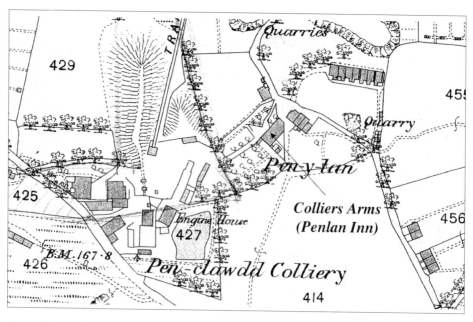

This 1878 map shows the location of the old Colliers Arms in the small community of Penylan. In 1826 it was called the Rising Sun, the later name change reflecting its closeness to Penclawdd Colliery. Thirsty miners were able to 'dampen the dust' very quickly after resurfacing! The pub was affectionately known as the 'Penlan Inn', but sadly its licence lapsed in 1874. The house still stands there today.

The Blue Anchor Inn in the 1960s. This old beerhouse was run by the Jenkins family in the late nineteenth century, when Swansea United's horse-drawn dray struggled up the hill with deliveries. John Jenkins was still landlord in 1906, aged seventy-seven, selling just two kils of beer a week. It became fully licensed in 1960 and a large function room was added, becoming a popular venue for parties. Sadly, the pub was demolished in 2004.

The Berthlwyd Inn, pictured here around the 1950s, was once a busy nineteenth-century beerhouse called the Colliers Arms. It was handily placed for the nearby Berthlwyd Colliery where 150 men worked, and its clubroom was used by the 'Alfreds' Lodge. The licensee in the early 1900s was John Davies, an engine driver whose wife looked after the pub. The pub's name changed to the Berthlwyd Inn in 1949 and it became a Chinese restaurant in 2004.

In 1850 a new alehouse licence was granted to Michael Evans at the 'Pumfald Inn' in the hamlet of the same name. The inn, now known as the Poundffald, was in the Evans family for nearly a century. The pub is at the site of an ancient pound for stray animals, and the circular stone *ffald* became the pub cellar and is now incorporated in the lounge area. The dual language name reminds us of the pub's location near the boundary of English and Welsh Gower. The Pumfald Gate was the scene of one of the Rebecca Riots in 1843 and the house may have been serving ale to travellers on this route from early times. Farmers reclaiming their animals would also have imbibed, had they any money left after paying their fines! This watercolour was painted by Tony Paultyn in the early 1980s, and the pound is at the rear, right.

Opposite above: This map shows the Poundffald Inn and Joiners Arms at Three Crosses in 1878. The road used to dog-leg around the Joiners, whose name probably derived from local timber working – note the sawpit alongside. The Joiners was licensed in 1864 and Philip Thomas was its first landlord. By 1921 the whole house was in a dilapidated state, the wall in front of the building was bulging forward in a dangerous manner and the pub was described as 'all to pieces'. Shortly afterwards, Swansea United Brewery rebuilt the pub and the road was straightened.

Opposite below: The Joiners Arms at Three Crosses in Trumans livery, after being rebuilt, 1930s.

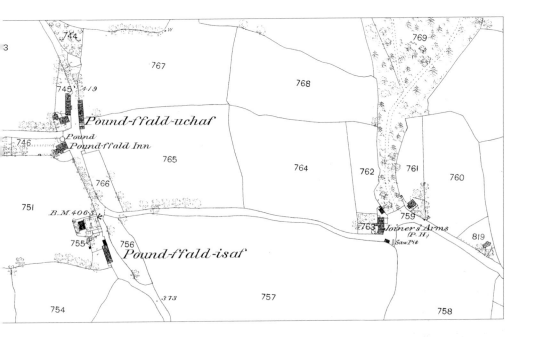

The Gower Inn, Gowerton, *c.* 1955. This busy crossroads is rarely traffic-free today! The original inn was built by John Hopkins in 1857, and is the oldest remaining pub in Gowerton (the earlier Railway Inn was built in 1853 but closed in the 1880s). In 1875, landlord Thomas Davies gave evidence at the inquest of a man killed on the nearby railway, saying the man was drinking at the inn some hours before he met his death. A licence transfer to James Williams was refused in 1895 as he'd previously been drunk at the London and North Western Hotel! The Gower Inn was rebuilt in 1907 and was renamed the Welsh Harp in 1969. Eight years later it became the Welcome to Gower, reflecting its position at the gateway to North Gower.

Buckley's Brewery took over the Gower Inn in 1896, their tenure lasting a century until they were taken over by Brains of Cardiff in 1997.

The London and North Western Hotel, Gowerton, with proprietor John Crowley, *c.* 1906. The hotel was built in 1884 as a 'coffee house', also providing accommodation for travellers, and a licence was granted to Thomas Jones in 1886. Its central location took advantage of the increased activity brought by local industry and the railway. Hancocks leased the hotel from 1919, purchasing it for £4,500 in 1923. The trade was very good at the time, averaging 536 barrels of beer and 300 gallons of wines and spirits per annum, although it later declined. In 1974, the hotel was granted an order for the playing of euchre, solo whist and phat – with restrictions regarding stakes. The front tower was removed in the 1970s and the name changed to the Ty Gwyn Mawr in 1991. The name changed back to the London and North Western in 2006, serving as a reminder of the pub's origins. Locals will be able to affectionately refer to the 'LN' once again.

Gowerton Fair day in 1912, with the Commercial Hotel on the left. This Victorian pub, near the railway station, was opened by David Jones in 1866 to provide refreshment for travellers and to service the growing commercial centre of Gower Road (now Gowerton). In 1908, the Commercial boasted a large clubroom and good stabling and coach house. Gowerton Mart was held for many years nearby and the Gowerton pubs were allowed to open between 11.00 a.m. and 6.00 p.m. on mart days. The bustling activity of the fair days and mart days, together with passengers from the railway, ensured plenty of trade.

The first day of Sunday opening at the Commercial after eighty years; 12 November 1961. From left to right: Jack (bach) Bowen, Bryn Thomas, Dai Miles, Phyllis Evans (landlady), John Rees, Bert Thomas, Owen Evans (landlord), PC Doug Spencer.

The old Found Out Inn in Dunvant, before it was demolished in 1964 to be replaced by today's modern building. The old stone inn was built in the mid-1850s by William Davies, who was apparently a chapel deacon! Originally called the Dunvant Inn, there are numerous stories about how it acquired its nickname. One is that thirsty colliers who called in after shift on pay days were 'found out' there by their wives and hauled off home before spending their pay-packets! The old pub has seen many characters, including Tom Williams who played rugby for Wales before the First World War. He was a member of the famed 'Terrible Eight' and became licensee in 1915. Another character in the 1930s was 'Roberts the Laverbread', one of the first makers of the famous seaweed delicacy. The pub's name changed officially in 1961.

The new Found Out Inn in 1964. The pub has long been a favourite watering hole for the Dunvant Male Choir.

The Railway Inn in Upper Killay is where we complete our journey, just along the Clyne Valley from where we started at Blackpill. The railway through the valley was constructed in 1864 and the inn was built by three local brothers in the same year. The picture shows the pub and Killay station platform before the railway disappeared in the Beeching cuts of the 1960s. A cycle track has replaced the railway lines but the pub remains, substantially unchanged since Victorian times. The atmosphere is timeless and one almost expects an express train to go thundering by at any moment. Its history reflects that of the Clyne valley and in 1872 an inquest was held there of William Barrett, one of two men killed in an accident at the nearby Rhydydefyd Colliery.

Opposite above: The Railway in Hancocks livery, *c.* 1930s. A century ago, the pub was owned by Swansea Old Brewery but in recent times the 'new' Swansea Brewing Co. of Bishopston has leased the pub. Despite winning CAMRA Pub of the Year awards, the pub has been under threat of demolition due to proposals to redevelop the site. It still survives however, the only pub in Upper Killay since the Plough and Horses closed over a century ago.

Opposite below: Swansea Brewing Co.'s ales, available at the Railway Inn in 2006. The beer mat celebrates the tenth anniversary of the brewery.

Swansea Brewing Company

1996 - 2006

SBC

Brewery Tap at The Joiners, Bishopston

Also available at the Railway, Killay

**Ten Years of Outstanding Beers
Brewed on Gower**

Other local titles published by Tempus

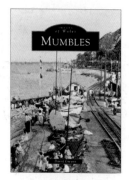

Mumbles
DAVID GWYNN

The famous Mumbles area of Swansea became a popular tourist destination after the first railway in the world to carry fare-paying passengers opened in 1807. It is now a thriving suburb, with pretty villages and attractive bays. Illustrated with over 200 old photographs and postcards, this book explores all aspects of life in the area. Images of working life, shops, schools and recreation create a vivid picture of times past.

0-7524 2858 6

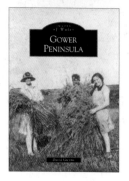

Gower Peninsula
DAVID GWYNN

This comprehensive collection of 200 images traces some of the changes that have taken place in the Gower Peninsula during the last century. The reader is taken on a tour of Gower when local craftsmen had their place in every village, and families and communities worked together. Each image is accompanied by supporting text providing a wealth of local colour and historical detail.

0 7524 2615 X

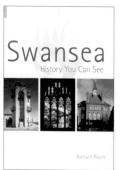

Swansea: History You Can See
RICHARD PORCH

The history of landmarks such as the Lockgate sculpture in Ferrara Quay, the copperworkers' township Hafod and the Whitford Point lighthouse – the only wave-washed lighthouse in Britain – is recorded in this A-Z of the people, buildings, industries and events that have shaped the city and county of Swansea.

0 7524 3076 9

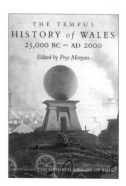

The Tempus History of Wales
PRYS MORGAN

Wales was at the heart of the Industrial Revolution, with towns like Merthyr Tydfil driving the engine of the British Empire. The cultural and social divide between modern, industrialised Wales and the traditional agricultural areas is explored within this comprehensive volume.

0 7524 1983 8

If you are interested in purchasing other books published by Tempus, or in case you have difficulty finding any Tempus books in your local bookshop, you can also place orders directly through our website

www.tempus-publishing.com